Innovation and Entrepreneurship

The Leader's Guide

Innovation and Entrepreneurship

The Leader's Guide

How to Innovate, Create New Markets and Achieve Growth Successfully

Simba K. Elisha

EXCELLER BOOKS®
A GLOBAL PRESS

Innovation and Entrepreneurship
The Leader's Guide
How to Innovate, Create New Markets and Achieve Growth Successfully

Cover by Exceller Books using resources from Pixabay.com

ISBN: 978-93-48892-76-8

First published in India in 2025 by Exceller Books,
An imprint of GE Group,
G1, Dream Apartment, Degree College Road, Belgharia,
Kolkata, 700056, India
www.excellerbooks.com

EXCELLER BOOKS®
A GLOBAL PRESS

Dedication

This book is dedicated to you, the agent of change. May the ideas in this book lift you up and help you succeed.

Acknowledgements

Writing this book was a collaborative effort, and I am deeply grateful to all who have contributed to its completion. My heartfelt thanks to my friend Shepherd Kagande, who continuously encouraged and pushed me to translate my thoughts and expertise into this book. Your support and belief have been invaluable. A special thanks to my dear friend Bridget and my brother Joseph and his family for their unwavering faith and support. Their love and patience gave me the strength to persevere through those days and nights of writing.

I am also profoundly grateful to Christensen C., Kim W., and Mauborgne R. Their influential work on innovation and entrepreneurship has greatly shaped the ideas presented in this book. I extend my sincere appreciation to my editor and publisher, whose expertise and dedication have brought this project to life. Your meticulous feedback was crucial in refining my work.

I acknowledge the business leaders, entrepreneurs, and innovators whose stories and experiences inspired this book. To my readers, I hope this book serves as a valuable resource on your journey to innovation and entrepreneurship.

And finally, to God, our Creator, be the Glory and Honour.

Contents

Chapter 1

The Fourth Industrial Revolution: Challenges and Opportunities

Historical Overview of Industrial Revolutions

The Fourth Industrial Revolution is profoundly reshaping individual lifestyles, cultures, organisational dynamics, and norms. We are witnessing how it has fundamentally altered our work processes, social interactions and how we buy and sell goods and services. We are witnessing a transformation across virtually every aspect of life and business. This revolution, part of a series of revolutions that began in the late 18th century, marks a significant evolution. The first industrial revolution shifted society from horsepower to mechanical power, and since then, progress has continued, and it will go on as long as there is life on this planet. Today, we find ourselves in the fourth phase, characterised by the emergence and convergence of exponential technologies such as artificial intelligence, smart machines and cloud computing. These technologies are enhancing human productivity across all sectors.

The first industrial revolution was from about 1760 to around 1840. Powered by the invention of the steam engine and the construction of railroads, it ushered in the printing press and other mechanical production tools and machines.

The second industrial revolution started in the late 19th century and into the early 20th century. The advances of that period made mass production possible, fostered by the advent of electricity and the assembly line. New industries emerged due to innovations in the transport, manufacturing and construction industries. As a result of mechanisation, the production of consumer goods began to move from cottages to factories. Scientific ways of management emerged to ensure efficiency in resource utilisation and optimise production processes. Citizens had more products at their disposal due to mass production and increased incomes.

In the US and other Western economies, industrialisation required a more educated workforce. Therefore, printed literature and textbooks encouraged compulsory education, which promoted literacy and extended learning beyond the world of wealthy upper-class citizens. Pamphlets, newsletters, and fliers spread information and ideas faster and farther than ever before.

The onset of the Third Industrial Revolution during the 1960s marked a pivotal moment in history. Often referred to as the computer or digital revolution, it was propelled by ground-breaking advances in the development of semiconductors. The proliferation of personal computing in the 1980s and the revolutionary impact of the internet and related information technologies in the 1990s gave Western Countries and the US industries competitive advantages across the globe. The internet and related digital connections unleashed massive potential for knowledge creation and diffusion, creating fertile opportunities and possibilities for knowledge-based innovations and entrepreneurship. Discerning individuals such as Steve Jobs, Bill Gates, Strive Masiyiwa and others astutely seized the burgeoning opportunities to establish knowledge-intensive enterprises. The strategic foresight of these and other visionaries laid the groundwork for the rise of knowledge as a quintessential factor of production.

Building on the foundations of the digital revolution, the fourth industrial revolution is characterised by a much more ubiquitous and mobile internet, smaller and more powerful sensors, and machine learning, all powered by artificial intelligence. Its scope is not limited to smart and connected machines and systems; it has a far wider scope. It began in the early 2000s with widespread adoption of digital technologies. Peter Drucker saw its emergence as the outcome of the integration of knowledge into tools, processes and products. He described it as an unprecedented industrial revolution that would exponentially enhance productivity, transform how knowledge is created and creatively applied in organisational innovation and entrepreneurship, and revolutionise management theory and practice.

The fourth industrial revolution has taken place, and there are waves of further breakthroughs in artificial intelligence, nanotechnology, renewables, and quantum computing. These breakthroughs are ushering in a post-industrial economy in which the importance of knowledge as a means of production is transforming the use of traditional factors of production, such as capital and labour, to control both societal and economic growth and progress. In advanced economies, including China, these technologies are triggering massive leaps in productivity, lowering production costs, and improving efficiencies.

The Impact of the Fourth Industrial Revolution

With these anticipated benefits, the Fourth Industrial Revolution has the potential to boost economic growth and address some of Africa's social and economic challenges. The technologies driving this revolution are profoundly transforming business management, organisation and customer interactions. Today, wealth can be generated with significantly fewer workers and less capital than two decades ago. Furthermore, new market entrants are rapidly achieving significant revenue milestones. For instance, Facebook, now Meta, reached $1 billion in annual revenue in six years, while Google did it in just five. In 2020, Tesla's market capitalisation surged by over $500 billion, making it as valuable as the nine largest global car companies combined, despite selling only a fraction of their volume.

With its massive benefits, the Fourth Industrial Revolution is unique and represents a significant departure from its predecessors in terms of the speed at which innovations are diffused and imitated globally. Unlike the previous three industrial revolutions, where innovations took decades to permeate across borders and for competitors to replicate, the pace of diffusion under 4IR is unprecedented. Emerging technologies are undoubtedly accelerating the speed and scale of change. When the speed and scale of change are accelerated, it has massive unintended implications for society as it adopts new innovations.

One key aspect driving this rapid diffusion is the democratisation of technology, which has lowered the barriers to accessing and adopting innovations. Open innovation models have accelerated the diffusion of technologies by promoting collaboration and knowledge sharing across organisations and industries. Android, the mobile operating system developed by Google, is an open-source platform running approximately 71.74% of the world's mobile devices as of mid-year 2024. Globalisation and interconnectedness facilitated by mobile internet, social media and artificial intelligence have created a hyper-connected global network, enabling information and innovations to spread across borders at unprecedented speed. In a matter of days, ground-breaking technologies developed in one part of the world can reach distant corners of the globe, transcending geographical barriers and time zones. The spinning jenny, invented by James Hargreaves in 1764 in England, revolutionised the textile industry by allowing one worker to spin multiple spools of thread simultaneously. The spread of the spinning jenny and similar mechanised spinning technologies took about 50 to 70 years to achieve global dissemination from its invention. Global adoption was a slow process, influenced by trade routes, colonisation and home-grown innovations.

Collaborative platforms, open-source software, and crowdsourcing initiatives allow innovators to leverage collective intelligence and accelerate the development and adoption of new technologies and the creation of new products and markets. Even less developed economies have greater access to cutting-edge technologies thanks to advancements in communication and transportation infrastructure. Innovations that were once exclusive to developed economies are now accessible to a much broader range of countries and businesses.

Moreover, the competitive pressure in today's global marketplace compels businesses to quickly adopt and adapt to emerging trends to maintain their competitive edge. In an environment where competitors can imitate innovations within hours, organisations must continuously innovate and evolve to stay ahead of the curve.

A Double-edged Sword for Lagging Economies

The faster diffusion of technologies during the Fourth Industrial Revolution presented a double-edged sword for less developed economies that were already lagging behind. On one hand, it provides unprecedented access to transformative technologies that can drive economic growth and development. On the other hand, it also increases the pressure on these economies to keep pace with rapid technological advancements to reduce the development and growth gap and become competitive global markets.

A notable example is the spread and use of smartphones and social media applications in regions without electricity, a cornerstone invention of the Second Industrial Revolution. This highlights a paradox wherein about 600 million people (43% of the total population) in Africa alone lack access to electricity. Globally, nearly 1.3 billion individuals, approximately 17% of the world's populace, still lack access to this fundamental resource. Of greater significance is the sad truth that half of the world's inhabitants, primarily residing in developing nations, are without internet connectivity, the flagship invention of the Third Industrial Revolution and the foundation for the fourth.

The pace of spread and adoption of 4IR technologies, if not well-addressed, is more likely to exacerbate existing and emerging challenges in Africa. They are creating first-mover advantages at the expense of laggards. There is a need to recognise and manage the negative impacts such advantages can have, particularly with regard to inequality, productivity and labour markets.

Expanding Business Operating Dimensions

Aside from speed, the fourth industrial revolution technologies, such as artificial intelligence (AI), are enabling businesses to develop AI-powered operational models. Algorithms and data analytics software are eliminating human and organisational bottlenecks in operations, leading to remarkable economies of scale and scope. Incorporating AI into business operations is driving scale to unprecedented levels, supporting businesses to offer a broader range of goods and services because an AI-powered operating model promotes faster learning and innovation.

According to economic theory, all businesses survive and thrive through continuous learning, which assists in achieving economies of scale and a sufficient scope. In this context, learning refers to the capability to improve and innovate continuously. AI-powered business and operating models enhance these capabilities, positioning businesses for sustained growth and competitiveness.

The value of a business is primarily shaped by its business model and operating model. The business model defines how the business creates and captures value, focusing on the strategy for competing and monetising its offerings. In contrast, the operating model delivers this value to customers.

Key elements of the operating model are organisational structure and managerial processes that enable and support production. These include primary operational activities, routines and practices that define the actual customer value. Every business operates along three critical dimensions:

1. Scale: A business becomes more profitable and sustainable when it can deliver value to as many customers as possible at the lowest possible cost.
2. Scope: This refers to the range of activities or variety of products and services a firm offers to customers. Successful businesses achieve efficiencies in scope by consistently and efficiently creating and delivering a wide range of products and services.
3. Learning: Continuous improvement through learning increases operating efficiency over time and facilitates the development of new products and services. Learning and innovation enable a business to navigate threats and exploit emerging opportunities.

Traditionally, each of these three operational dimensions – scale, scope, and learning – could only be expanded up to a certain critical point. Beyond this limit, increasing them would result in increased operational complexity, leading to inefficiencies, diseconomies of scale and scope, and ultimately diminishing returns. This was primarily because traditional operating models relied on human capacities and physical assets, which have inherent constraints.

For example, a restaurant can only serve a limited number of customers before reaching its maximum capacity and overwhelming its staff. Similarly, a factory has a finite production capacity. To scale beyond these limits, businesses should invest in additional assets and hire more personnel. These constraints illustrate the limitations of traditional operating models that rely on human and physical resources.

These constraints ultimately lead to diminishing returns as scale and scope increase.

Deploying algorithms in designing software and data-driven operating models is enabling businesses to scale beyond traditional operational constraints, thus eliminating human and organisational bottlenecks from the critical path of delivering value to customers. For example, a restaurant can develop a software application that allows customers to make orders online and have home deliveries, enabling a restaurant to serve more customers than its tables can accommodate.

Tech giants like Google, Amazon, and Ant Financial have attained unprecedented levels of scalability, achieved a vastly broader scope, and are rapidly learning and adapting compared to traditional businesses. How many products are on Amazon? How many people use Google? Internet surfing is known as googling. This success is largely due to embedding AI and software in their operating models. AI-powered operating models enable an organisation to:

1. Connect complementary activities, processes and partners, offering numerous potential combinations and possibilities for increasing scale and scope.
2. Interact and communicate at zero marginal cost with virtually unlimited networked partners and customers.
3. Learn and improve operational performance over time as they learn from data.

The fourth industrial revolution brought technology, business strategy, and operations closer together through innovations in business models and operating models. This integration is a complex aspect of digital and AI transformation. It fundamentally revolutionises how organisations operate, including in terms of management and leadership. Business model and operating model innovations that result from embedding AI tools and systems within key operational activities and processes that create and deliver customer value are driving business scale, scope and learning beyond traditional constraints in the following ways:

1. Improving Scalability: Digitisation means automation, which allows companies to avoid diminishing returns to scale. The automation of tasks and processes through machine learning and robotic algorithms supports the handling of repetitive and time-consuming tasks with efficiency and accuracy that would otherwise require significant human effort. This allows an organisation to manage larger volumes of work without proportional increases in human resources and capital investments and serve a large number of customers at a low cost. AI-driven automation streamlines operations, increases productivity and facilitates growth without compromising quality.
2. Broadens Business Scope: By leveraging advanced algorithms to process and analyse vast amounts of data, AI uncovers patterns, correlations and insights that may not be apparent through manual analysis. This enables firms to gain a deeper understanding of their customers, market trends, and business dynamics. These data-driven insights empower organisations to make more informed decisions, identify new market opportunities and develop a variety of innovative products and services to address customer pain points.
3. Create Strong Learning Effects: AI facilitates continuous learning within an organisation by leveraging data to improve performance and optimise processes. AI algorithms can learn from historical data, real-time feedback, and iterative cycles to enhance their accuracy and predictive capabilities. This learning ability allows organisations to adapt and optimise their operations based on changing circumstances. AI-driven learning enables mass customisation and delivers targeted recommendations. This data-driven learning helps identify areas for improvement, refine business strategies,

and make data-driven decisions. Additionally, AI facilitates organisational learning by capturing and sharing knowledge across teams, departments, and business units.

The more a business can drive scale, scope, and learning, the greater its value. Digital businesses have marginal costs that tend toward zero and leverage highly competitive markets via digital platforms, which results in lower prices. Innovative goods and services from the fourth industrial revolution boast significantly higher functionality and quality yet are delivered in fundamentally different markets from those we traditionally measure.

Many new goods and services are "non-rival" and have zero marginal costs. Tech companies like Instagram and WhatsApp required minimal financial capital to start, illustrating a shift in the role of financial capital and business scaling in the context of the fourth industrial revolution. This new environment allows businesses to leverage digital technology to scale rapidly and efficiently, significantly reducing the traditional costs associated with growth.

Increasing returns to scale afforded by 4IR technologies not only encourages scaling but also drives transformative changes across economies. The question is: How can African businesses leverage these advantages by focusing on automation and minimising marginal costs to achieve exponential growth and sustained competitiveness? What does it take to remove the digital divide and infrastructure limitations that are hindering widespread adoption? A suppressed, widespread adoption inhibits less developed economies from leveraging technology advancements for economic growth and prosperity, thus exacerbating existing inequalities.

Klaus Schwab, founder and Executive Chairman of the World Economic Forum, summed up the impact of the fourth industrial revolution as follows:

1. It provides an opportunity to address the unmet needs of the marginalised and excluded people by integrating them into the global economy. Empowering and connecting individuals and communities drives additional demand for existing products and services, thus promoting growth and prosperity.
2. The Fourth Industrial Revolution significantly enhances our ability to profitably address existing and emerging challenges, such as climate change, thereby boosting potential economic growth and social development.
3. To capture the full value and realise the efficiencies that digital capabilities offer, entirely new economic and organisational structures are required because the competitive rules of the Fourth Industrial Revolution differ significantly from those of previous periods.

Promoting growth and prosperity through the adoption of 4IR technologies, businesses and governments must be at the frontier of innovation in all its forms. Strategies that primarily focus on reducing costs are now less effective than those that are based on offering products and services in more innovative ways. Public and private organisations must recognise the need to focus on building innovation ecosystems accordingly.

The challenge for leaders is keeping up with the rapidly changing landscape. Given the unprecedented impact these changes are having on consumption, investment, productivity, and growth patterns, most leaders understand that something needs to be done but do not know what or how to do it.

Balancing Labour Supply and Demand

The Fourth Industrial Revolution (4IR) presents both a paradoxical challenge and a significant opportunity for companies, economies and societies. Smart machines and artificial intelligence are predicted to offer unprecedented productivity gains and production efficiencies, supporting exponential growth and economic development. However, these advancements are coming at a considerable social and economic cost.

Digitalisation and industrial automation are replacing certain human tasks, leading to job displacements across virtually all sectors. Many different categories of work, particularly those that involve mechanically repetitive and precise manual labour, are being automated. As computing power continues to grow exponentially, the work of professionals, such as lawyers, financial analysts, doctors, journalists, accountants, insurance underwriters, and librarians, is also becoming partly or completely automated. Human jobs are being taken over by AI-powered machines that perform cognitive functions more effectively than humans.

Research has shown that, globally, employment has been growing in high-income cognitive and creative jobs and low-income manual occupations but greatly diminishing for middle-income routine and repetitive jobs in the wake of smart machines and automation. Faced with emerging technologies, the challenge for companies is not to protect human workers from these advancements but to adopt these technologies and remain relevant in the market. Not adopting Fourth Industrial Revolution (4IR) technologies in the name of saving jobs is a kiss of death because modernisation is essential. Failure to modernise will inevitably lead to obsolescence. Without modern production systems, businesses will inevitably become inefficient and less competitive globally, ultimately going out of business and leading to even greater job losses.

Advances in 4IR technologies have indeed created new jobs that did not exist a decade ago, and they are expected to generate more jobs in the future that we cannot yet imagine. As economies and societies undergo digital transformation, the common response to job threats at the organisational level is upskilling and reskilling. These measures — retraining, upskilling, and reskilling — are supply-side interventions; they do not create new jobs. They simply ensure the supply-side readiness necessary for transitioning workers to a new job. They guarantee that workers are prepared for new roles and responsibilities in a modernised workplace.

Therefore, the question remains: Where will the new jobs come from, and who will create the new institutions that will generate these jobs? The answer to these questions lies in demand-side interventions. Job-creating demand-side interventions are necessary to ensure that jobs will be available for displaced employees, matching the supply-side readiness. Currently, much effort is focused on supply-side interventions, with insufficient attention to the demand side. Without balancing both aspects, it is impossible to fully exploit and benefit from the technological revolution while minimising its negative social and economic impacts.

Now Is the Time to Act

Balancing supply and demand has sparked a renewed interest in two key demand-side interventions: innovation and entrepreneurship. These concepts are not new. Since the days of Joseph Schumpeter, innovation and entrepreneurship have been recognised as the true drivers of economic growth and prosperity. Economists and business managers unanimously agree that sustainable growth comes from creating rather than merely competing. In Africa, there is more room to create new institutions, new products and services than competing in the existing and mostly saturated markets. The several challenges faced in all sectors of the economy and society represent opportunities for new market creation.

Now is the time for us to apply the lessons we have learned from South Korea, Singapore, Malaysia and China. These economies have transformed their growth trajectories by adopting an innovation-led economic growth model. This model emphasises innovation and entrepreneurship as the key drivers of growth and prosperity for both companies and societies. In an innovation-led growth model, entrepreneurship and innovation take centre stage in creating new products, services, processes and business models that enhance productivity, create new markets and jobs, increase industry competitiveness and generate new economic value. By following this approach, we can similarly elevate Africa's economic growth and prosperity.

China's "Made in China 2025" is one of the successful innovation-led growth initiatives that has made China one of the global economic powerhouses. There are many other examples that illustrate how companies, countries and regions can leverage innovation to achieve sustained economic growth, job creation, and global competitiveness. In today's world, innovation is a must. The capacity to innovate is the critical determinant of an organisation's future prosperity and influence. Therefore, it is only through innovation and entrepreneurship that Africa can deal with rising economic inequalities and socio-political unrest.

Change is happening now, and greater change is expected. Whether we lay the foundations for a better and prosperous Africa depends largely on the actions we take or do not take and the strategies we implement or do not implement. Leaders across all sectors, including business, government and civil society, must understand the changes underway and the urgent need to rethink current economic, social and political systems to respond to the fourth industrial revolution.

At the national and firm level, the requisite institutional framework to govern the diffusion of innovation and mitigate the impact is inadequate at best and, at worst, absent altogether, and that needs to be changed. Given that many sub-Saharan African countries are barely able to provide their growing populations with the most basic services, such as health care and education, Africa cannot afford to remain behind the rest of the world any longer. The time to act is now because lagging will further exacerbate the developmental challenges and risks for future generations. In the aftermath of the COVID-19 pandemic, poverty and inequality are still widespread. Africa's economic growth has been deemed insufficient by the World Bank to alleviate extreme poverty or promote shared prosperity in the long term.

Chapter 2

Rising Importance of Innovation and Entrepreneurship

In 2014, Sub-Saharan Africa's GDP per capita peaked at $1,936, sparking optimism among analysts and leaders about the region's future. Advances in the Fourth Industrial Revolution (4IR) technologies, such as artificial intelligence, the Internet of Things (IoTs), and blockchain, were seen as game changers. These technologies were expected to disrupt traditional industries and job markets and were predicted to result in unprecedented opportunities for exponential growth and economic development. Many believed Africa could surpass the Asian tigers in terms of growth and development.

However, nearly a decade later, Africa's GDP per capita declined by more than 10%, now standing at about $1,700 in the post-Covid era, while GDP per capita across the rest of the world increased by nearly 15% during the same period. In a 2023 Bloomberg article titled *"Africa Rising No More: Economic Turmoil and Shrinking Opportunities Put the Continent at Risk,"* Javier Blas paints a bleak picture of the region's future. He argues that Africa's reliance on a commodity-led growth model is a significant factor in its economic problems, as it leaves the economy vulnerable to price fluctuations. Javier's comments are not far from the truth. The heightened global tensions experienced soon after the COVID-19 pandemic witnessed commodity prices not keeping pace with inflation, adversely affecting the continent's terms of trade. We have literally left the destiny of our economies to be decided by forces beyond our control. With the population growing at a steady annual rate of 2.5%, Africa needs to take the wheel of control and establish a new growth trajectory.

The previous chapter outlined the challenges and opportunities the Fourth Industrial Revolution (4IR) presents for companies, economies, and society. The challenges may further exacerbate Africa's problems if they are not well addressed and opportunities are not seized and exploited to turn around the economic and social fortunes of the continent. Without a doubt, the Fourth Industrial Revolution presents African economies with a distinctive opportunity to creatively adopt externally developed technologies and propel forward inclusive growth and sustainable development in innovative ways.

The rapid diffusion of 4IR technologies and the increasing returns to scale they afford, coupled with a young-educated population, provide Africa with an unrivalled opportunity to leapfrog traditional stages of development. But first, we need a paradigm shift. We need to start by changing our perspective on the lagging position. Rather than seeing lagging as a hindrance, governments, businesses and entrepreneurs should embrace it as a strategic advantage to sense and seize new growth opportunities. This shift in perspectives opens our minds to existing opportunities and inspires many to explore and exploit new and efficient economic growth trajectories without incurring the full costs and risks associated with investing in new technologies.

In the 1980s, economists coined the term "leapfrogging" to describe a phenomenon where companies and economies experience rapid growth and development. This strategy involves latecomers or laggards leveraging new technologies and innovative solutions to propel themselves forward, bypassing inefficient and costly intermediate stages of development. A prime illustration of leapfrogging's impact on economic development and prosperity is found in the Asian Tigers: Hong Kong, Singapore, South Korea, and

Taiwan. These nations achieved remarkable economic growth by sidestepping traditional developmental stages in the latter half of the 20th century. Rather than following the conventional path of industrialisation seen in Western countries, they prioritised the adoption of advanced technologies and innovative production methods.

Africa has leveraged remarkable technological advancements during the third industrial revolution and paved the way for leapfrogging in multiple sectors. These innovations are a testament to the potential of Africa's tech industry and its ability to push beyond limitations and challenges. During the late 1900s, several governments chose to skip the conventional landline telephone systems and instead adopted the new mobile telecommunications technologies. The instances mentioned below are also convincing proofs of the possibility of leapfrogging in Africa.

1. *Mobile Banking*

M-Pesa in Mozambique and Kenya and Ecocash in Zimbabwe epitomise a revolutionary leap in the financial sector. These mobile money platforms capitalised on Africa's impressive mobile phone penetration rates. They were conceived to enable users to effortlessly transfer money and conduct transactions via mobile phones, circumventing the necessity for conventional banking infrastructure. This ground-breaking innovation has notably heightened financial inclusivity, particularly among low-income and rural demographics, by granting access to fundamental financial services without the prerequisite bank account.

2. *E-commerce*

Nigeria's rapidly growing e-commerce sector exemplifies Africa's capacity for leapfrogging. Despite facing hurdles like inadequate physical infrastructure and logistical complexities, platforms like Jumia and Konga have thrived, granting countless consumers access to diverse goods and services online. This shift away from conventional retail models holds promise for bolstering economic expansion and enhancing consumer accessibility to products and services throughout the continent. Notably, Africa's e-commerce has sustained a robust 17% compound annual growth rate (CAGR) since 2021, as reported by the International Trade Administration (https://www.trade.gov/rise-ecommerce-africa). In early 2024, Amazon was launched in the South African market, where Chinese e-commerce companies Temu and Shein have met with wonderful success.

Broadening Perspectives on Entrepreneurship and Innovation

Leapfrogging is not an automatic process; it requires a holistic approach that addresses multiple dimensions of development. World Bank's list of the critical conditions required to accelerate Africa's economic development and achieve long-term prosperity include robust human capital development and a vibrant innovation and entrepreneurship ecosystem. And that is the subject matter of this book: innovation and entrepreneurship. You may ask: Why another book on innovation and entrepreneurship? To answer that question, we need to broaden our perspective on the vast opportunities available for entrepreneurship and innovation. We shall begin by establishing clear operational definitions of innovation and entrepreneurship and recognise their inherent interconnectedness.

Until now, we have used the terms entrepreneurship and innovation loosely and often interchangeably. This mirrors their usage in everyday life. We use words based on the particular images and ideas they evoke in our minds. Therefore, refining our understanding of these concepts is crucial to understanding the rising importance of innovation and entrepreneurship for economic growth and social development. By doing so, we can better articulate what drives innovation and how to effectively harness it to promote entrepreneurship.

What Is Innovation?

Innovation is both a process and the outcome of that process. It is the creative process by which entrepreneurs exploit change or challenges as an entrepreneurial opportunity to create new value. Innovation encompasses knowledge-based activities such as idea generation, imagination, and conceptualisation. It results from the application, sharing and use of knowledge to develop new products, services, processes and strategies for growing businesses, industries, and regions. There are three main types of innovation: sustaining innovation, efficiency innovation, and market-creating innovation. Each type plays a unique role in the growth and development of organisations. The lack of market-creating innovation is a primary cause of many challenges in Africa, making it the focal point of this book. Market-creating innovation generates real value for specific customers or users, fuelling a country's economic engine. In *"The Prosperity Paradox: How Innovation Can Lift Nations out of Poverty."* Christensen, Ojomo, and Dillon point out that market-creating innovations yield three distinct outcomes:

1. Job Creation: These innovations generate employment opportunities as an increasing number of people are needed to manufacture, market, distribute, and sell new products and services. Job creation is a critical factor in assessing a country's prosperity.
2. Profit Generation: They generate profits across a broad segment of the population. These profits often fund essential public services such as education, infrastructure, and healthcare.
3. Cultural Transformation: Market-creating innovations have the potential to transform the culture of entire societies. Many developed Western countries,

including the United States, were once poor, corrupt, and poorly governed. However, the proliferation of market-creating innovations since the first Industrial Revolution initiated a process that significantly transformed these economies.

The concept of innovation as a process has enabled the observation, study and analysis of its constituent parts, leading to the development of systematic innovation models. This has demystified innovation, transforming it into a discipline that can be learned and practised by individuals. Consequently, innovation is no longer seen as merely the result of serendipitous encounters or eureka moments. Research has shown that innovative organisations and individuals are highly strategic in their approach, viewing innovation-led growth as critical and deliberately pursuing it.

What Is Entrepreneurship?

Entrepreneurship, on the other hand, is the commercialisation of innovative outcomes to develop business enterprises. Innovation is a tool or instrument in the hands of an entrepreneur. Entrepreneurship leads to the creation of new enterprises that generate economic value and social impact. Everyone who starts a small business is identified as an entrepreneur. However, entrepreneurship is deeper than simply starting small businesses; it is about creating and delivering new economic and social value. It is about creating something different rather than copying and pasting a corner shop. Entrepreneurs transmute values and impact societies. Small and new are not the defining characteristics of entrepreneurship; big businesses are also entrepreneurial.

From a functional perspective, entrepreneurship defines how dynamic actors (entrepreneurs) make key decisions about investments, production, consumption and development. They reallocate national resources to areas where they have a greater impact. Entrepreneurs, whether running their own businesses or working within existing organisations, influence the pace of economic and technological advancement and the structural transformation of organisations, sectors and economies. These actors contribute to spreading knowledge by commercialising inventions and discoveries, thereby stimulating further innovations and initiating cycles of economic growth.

Innovation and Entrepreneurship in the Knowledge Society

Innovation, entrepreneurship and knowledge are closely intertwined, with each driving and reinforcing the other. Knowledge, however, stands out as the fundamental source and resource for both innovation and entrepreneurship, serving as a strategic asset that shapes the competitiveness and prosperity of businesses and nations alike. Knowledge, in this context, goes beyond mere know-what, know-why, and know-how; it encompasses the capacity of individuals or organisations to produce and deliver new customer value outcomes.

Competitive advantages derived from tangible assets are becoming increasingly temporary in today's hostile markets. Instead, knowledge-based intangible assets are now the source of a sustainable competitive edge. Modern strategies for wealth generation and growth for both economies and businesses have shifted from reliance on physical assets to prioritising intangible assets, also known as intellectual capital. Thus, learning is an integral part of the economic growth and survival formula.

As a result, different stages of the innovation and entrepreneurship process are supported by specific learning behaviours. Learning enables individuals and organisations to stay abreast of emerging technologies and other market changes and to respond accordingly. It exposes entrepreneurs and innovators to diverse perspectives, ideas, and experiences, fuelling creative problem-solving and critical thinking. It equips them with the capacity and ability to tackle complex social and economic challenges.

Moving to New Organisational and Industry Dynamics

The increasing role of knowledge in economic activities provides a fertile ground for discovering new marketable opportunities for discerning individuals and organisations. Economic growth and progress in the knowledge society depend largely on the presence of a substantial number of knowledge workers and entrepreneurs. These individuals are pivotal in expanding the organisational knowledge base, which is essential for fostering creativity, innovation and entrepreneurship. Knowledge workers and entrepreneurs are the primary drivers of innovation and the commercialisation of new and original ideas.

With estimates suggesting that 70 per cent to 80 per cent of organisational knowledge is contained within the minds of its workers, the rise in the significance of knowledge has fundamentally altered the role of labour and capital in driving economic growth, promoting wealth creation and enhancing industry competitiveness. As a result, organisational design and structure have transformed to focus more on human capital development and knowledge management strategies to unlock creativity. Knowledge management capabilities support and facilitate social activities involved in the exploration and exploitation of growth opportunities. The challenge for leadership and management is to provide a conducive environment in the workplace for dreaming, exploring, co-creating and experimenting.

The shifts brought about by the ascendency of knowledge in economic and social activities represent a profound transformation in organisational and industry dynamics, departing from the traditional focus on tangible assets and eliminating waste in resource utilisation that defined the business and economic systems in the previous era to today's knowledge-based systems. During the previous industrial era, the defining attributes which shaped business operations centred on:

1. Physical Resources: Access to raw materials and physical resources held significant strategic importance. Firms that owned and controlled physical resources asserted market dominance. Most are still tied to these assets, which are now good for the museum, blaming the new models for their demise.
2. Capital Investment: Physical assets were held in high esteem because success hinged on access to capital and physical assets like factories and advanced machinery. Heavy investments in infrastructure, machinery, and factories were necessary for mass production. Market saturation was often the goal, requiring effective marketing and sales strategies. Efficient management of supply chains and distribution channels was imperative to maximise efficiency, a vital contributor to competitive advantage.
3. Manual Labour: Human labour primarily focused on easily replaceable physical tasks and manual skills. The competition revolved around optimising human resource utilisation. Lower labour costs and enhanced productivity directly influenced competitive positioning.
4. Production Efficiency: Companies that could achieve higher production efficiency at lower costs gained a competitive edge. Emphasising mass production and standardisation facilitated consistency, efficiency, and predictability in managing large-scale production and distribution.

While competition in the industrial era focused on tangible assets and production efficiencies, the knowledge age emphasises intangible assets, mass customisation, and the strategic use of information as the foundation for market innovation.

The rise in the significance of knowledge, coupled with the advances in machine learning and artificial intelligence, has transformed the structure of organisations and how they operate. Sustainable competitive advantage now hinges on the organisation's ability to harness and leverage knowledge effectively, fostering a culture of turning knowledge into products, services and strategies to respond to changing market forces. Competition now revolves around intangible assets and the strategic use of information.

Key factors defining the modern knowledge-based economy include:

1. *Intangible Assets*

Also known as intellectual capital (IC), intangibles such as human imagination, ideas and intuition are the major sources of wealth creation and competitive advantage. It encompasses the collective knowledge and competencies that define how other factors of production are combined and transformed into processes, products or services that drive organisational performance and growth. Intellectual capital exists in people, relationships, processes, and interactions that are supported and enabled by the organisational structure and culture. The effect of IC on organisational performance is seen in innovation capacity and entrepreneurship. Intellectual assets are unique to the organisation and difficult for competitors to replicate, such as proprietary technologies, patents, brand identity and deep relationships built on trust. Organisations with highly skilled and creative talent have a competitive edge rather than those with heavy investments in physical assets.

2. *Human Capital Investments*

The foundational base of a knowledge economy is characterised by education, training, absorptive capacity, prior knowledge, knowledge flow, and technological knowledge transfer. Citizens must engage in continuous and lifelong learning to build a workforce capable of incorporating, managing, and supporting technological, social, and innovation capabilities.

The ongoing Fourth Industrial Revolution (4IR), coupled with globalisation, is intensifying environmental turbulence, competition and uncertainty, forcing individuals and organisations to continuously learn to remain competitive and relevant. Learning enables the crafting of innovative strategies that not only enable creative responses to changes in the environment and societal pressures but also consider the needs and expectations of various stakeholders in creating sustainable competitive advantage. Intangible-knowledge-based assets have emerged as the most strategically significant sources of sustainable competitive advantage. A sustainable competitive edge comes from what the organisation knows, how it is using what it knows and how fast it can know something new, accentuating the importance of human capital and intellectual property.

Constant and rapid change means businesses must constantly update their knowledge and skills to stay competitive. Learning also enhances problem-solving abilities, allowing businesses to respond effectively to challenges and opportunities. By prioritising ongoing education and skill development, businesses can drive sustainable growth, improve operational efficiency and maintain a competitive edge. A culture of continuous learning, which involves both formal training and informal knowledge sharing, feeds back into continuous innovation and entrepreneurship.

3. *Agile and Flexible Organisations*

Advances in AI, machine learning, and data analytics allow effective knowledge management to support and enable data-based decision-making, empowering organisations to be agile and flexible.

Agility refers to the ability of an organisation to rapidly respond to changes in the market environment. It involves quick decision-making and the capacity to implement changes swiftly.

Flexibility is the capability of an organisation to adjust its processes, structures, and strategies for mass customisation. It encompasses the proactive decision-making and adaptability of an organisation's resources and workflows to meet changing customer demands.

4. *Networks and Collaboration*

In an interconnected society, networks and collaboration are essential not only for organisations but also for individuals. In addition to industry analysis, organisations must conduct network analysis to identify possible internal or external partners to collaborate with in enhancing innovation, competitiveness, and market expansion. Collaboration brings diverse ideas, perspectives and resources and enables access to specialised skills and technologies that can reduce costs through shared resources and mitigate risks by distributing them across ecosystem partners. Knowledge sharing within networks keeps businesses updated on emerging trends and fosters continuous improvement. Additionally, collaboration builds trust, strengthens reputation, and promotes employee engagement and productivity. Effective networks and collaboration drive sustained business growth and success.

Organisations are now structured to thrive in an environment shaped by digital networks, artificial intelligence and data analytics. Modern organisational design focuses on leveraging knowledge and information to support innovation and entrepreneurship, forming the foundation for sustainable growth. At the heart of societal advancement and economic development are innovation and entrepreneurship.

Entrepreneurs and innovators operate within specific social and economic contexts. At the national level, public policy significantly influences how they respond to opportunities, challenges, and risks. To kindle and support the entrepreneurial spirit, governments must prioritise investments in developing the national knowledge base, cultivate relevant markets and enact legal frameworks that safeguard intellectual property rights.

At the organisational level, innovation and entrepreneurship require supportive and well-aligned organisational processes, structures and culture. In the era of networks and hyper-connectivity, social interactions occur randomly and at high speeds, resulting in constantly changing market conditions. Conventional organisational processes for strategic planning, goal-setting, self-evaluation and course correction were not designed to support and enable change but rather to preserve the current order by maintaining consistency and predictability. Consequently, these processes operate on socially constructed milestones with annual or quarterly checkpoints. Innovation is about effecting change rather than maintaining the status quo; therefore, it requires new approaches and systems.

Creativity and learning occur suddenly when a previously unknown solution to a problem creates a new, unexpected outcome. Therefore, leadership is responsible for ensuring that organisational structures, processes, and systems are in place to capture these learning outcomes. By doing so, they can develop strategies and responses that drive growth and create multiple layers of competitive advantage.

Challenge for Leaders

Despite gaining political independence, most African countries are still running on resource-based growth models that have proven detrimental to the economy. They have brought development and growth but are perpetuating inequality and exclusion at the expense of inclusive growth and prosperity. Despite being endowed with abundant natural and human resources, Africa grapples with pervasive poverty, underdevelopment, political instability, and social turmoil instead of reaping the benefits of its resource wealth.

A new generation of African leaders is challenging this status quo and demanding a paradigm shift. Africa's overreliance on extractive industries has left it economically vulnerable. It is impeding diversification efforts, stifling industrialisation and service sector growth, exacerbating inequality, and incentivising corruption and insurgency.

The challenge for those in management and leadership is to rethink their styles, attitudes, and beliefs with the goal of transforming their organisations' structures, production systems, and processes. They must embrace change rather than avoid it and inspire their teams to initiate and exploit opportunities for change. This involves adopting mindsets, strategies and policies that promote and enable innovation and entrepreneurship.

Innovation and entrepreneurship are inherently social processes that require learning, exploration, agility, flexibility, collaboration, and experimentation to be embedded within an organisation's structure, culture and processes. With the intensification of competition across all sectors due to globalisation, the survival and success of organisations and economies increasingly hinge on their ability to innovate and create new markets.

For Africa to adapt to and adopt new structural patterns that will drive economic growth and prosperity, it needs to harness the ideas and creativity of its people. Local research and organisational efforts are essential in rethinking economic and organisational theories, models, policies and regulations. This includes redefining business models, social processes and personal well-being to align with the demands of the new economy.

To achieve leapfrogging, it is crucial to develop and implement regionally adapted innovations that facilitate a swift transition from resource-based to innovation-led growth models. These innovations need to be locally sourced and tailored for Africa. Today, leaders and entrepreneurs face the challenge of navigating a rapidly evolving landscape where traditional growth models and strategies are falling short.

This book is for innovators, entrepreneurs, and leaders across the private and public sectors who are driving change and seeking effective ways to transform their communities and organisations. Its primary aim is to guide change-makers in identifying existing and emerging economic and social challenges as opportunities for creating new markets, products, and services.

Within these pages, you will find insights on creating new markets and establishing organisations that not only generate new jobs but also stimulate economic growth and foster shared prosperity. The focus is to inspire the development of innovative solutions to everyday problems, thereby contributing to sustainable development and societal advancement.

The remainder of this book is structured into five chapters. Here is a comprehensive outline of what lies ahead:

- Chapter 3 delves into essential entrepreneurial mindsets, perspectives, and behaviours needed to drive and lead transformative change. Leading with the right mindset and perspective sets the stage for promoting market-creating innovation and entrepreneurship. This foundation is crucial for empowering organisations to creatively confront their most significant challenges and effectively initiate, manage, and implement change.
- Chapter 4 expands on current perspectives of innovation and explores two primary pathways to market-creating innovation: disruptive and non-disruptive. It aims to help readers grasp the essence of the problems they

intend to solve and identify the appropriate pathway to address these challenges.

- Chapter 5 lays the groundwork for uncovering identified entrepreneurial opportunities. It offers insights into exposing industry assumptions that obscure market-creating prospects. The chapter also guides readers on developing a business model designed to unlock the potential of identified opportunities by assessing and challenging these assumptions.
- Chapter 6 discusses three key enablers crucial for effective strategy execution: internal resources and capabilities, resourcefulness and a growth mindset. These enablers are essential for translating strategies and tactics devised to unlock opportunities into actionable steps that bring products or services to market.
- And finally, chapter 7 concludes by highlighting the immense potential for market-creating innovations in Africa. It emphasises the importance of collective effort and determination in pursuing these opportunities. By leveraging emerging technologies to address both existing but unexplored and emerging challenges, we can chart a new growth trajectory through market-creating innovations and build the future we want.

Chapter 3

Entrepreneurial Mindset and Perspectives

For too long, Africa has been hampered by self-sabotaging perspectives that have stifled entrepreneurship and perpetuated underdevelopment across the continent. For decades, the common approach to addressing Africa's social and economic challenges has focused on "alleviating poverty". Governments, the private sector, including non-governmental organisations and multilateral institutions such as the World Bank, have operated with the same narrative. However, Christensen C, Ojomo E. and Dillon K. challenged this view in their book, *The Prosperity Paradox: How Innovation Can Lift Nations out of Poverty*. They argued that Africa's problems should be tackled from the perspective of "creating prosperity and growth" rather than "alleviating poverty". They defined prosperity not merely as wealth but as the improvement of economic, social, and political well-being across entire regions.

Christensen et al. pointed out that framing the issue as poverty alleviation fails to motivate decision-makers to ask the critical question: What are the root causes of poverty? Consequently, interventions designed to "alleviate poverty" typically address only the symptoms of poverty, such as malnutrition, poor education and high mortality rates, leaving the roots intact. They concluded that while "injecting resources and goodwill" may provide short-term relief, it fails to address the systemic issues causing poverty.

Operating with this flawed perspective, over US$1.2 trillion has been poured into Africa's development assistance over the past three decades. Yet, the continent has little to show for it. Why? It is because the focus was on alleviating poverty rather than creating prosperity. While there has been some success in alleviating poverty, the solutions have not been sustainable. As the population continues to grow, more aid is needed. Coupled with the effects of natural disasters and political instability, even more aid will continue to be required to alleviate poverty. Going forward, we must shift from channelling resources toward short-term solutions to strategies aimed at sustainable economic development. This shift demands a change in perspectives and mindsets because prosperity is holistic progress, encompassing a country's economic, social, and political dimensions. That is the reason why this book is relevant for leaders in both the public and private sectors of the economy. Entrepreneurship and innovation not only drive economic growth but also uplift entire communities by generating jobs, increasing productivity, and improving infrastructure.

This chapter explores the entrepreneurial mindsets and perspectives that empower individuals and organisations to foster prosperity by creatively addressing the most pressing social and economic challenges. Its purpose is to lay the groundwork for initiating, managing, and implementing change required to promote prosperity and growth. Shifting from poverty alleviation to promoting prosperity requires a change in perspectives that fundamentally alters how challenges are approached and solved. Focusing solely on poverty alleviation results in short-term solutions, such as aid and relief programs. Embracing a prosperity-driven mindset broadens our toll-kit to include sustainable, innovation-led growth and market creation, leading to economic resilience. This shift empowers local communities to take ownership of their economic development, promoting job creation and broader socio-economic improvements.

A focus on prosperity changes success metrics from simple poverty reduction to job creation, infrastructure development, and overall social well-being. It inspires collaboration among governments, private sectors, and international institutions, driving policies that support entrepreneurship and sustainable growth. By viewing challenges through the lens of promoting prosperity, leaders can create long-term strategies that lead to holistic, self-sustaining progress, ultimately improving economic, social, and political stability across regions.

Entrepreneurship as Emergence

The first and key perspective shift in promoting prosperity is understanding entrepreneurship as an emergent property. The goal of entrepreneurship is to establish a new economic and social order. This is a key perspective shift because it highlights how innovation and entrepreneurial opportunities arise from the non-linear interactions, unpredictable collective actions and dynamics within an organisation or society rather than being solely driven by linear individual efforts or isolated initiatives. These non-linear and unpredictable interactions and actions of different actors mean entrepreneurship is a process of constantly navigating unfolding equivocal situations. Equivocal situations are characterised by a lack of clear information, making decision-making and action-taking very challenging due to high uncertainty and ambiguity. Ambiguity introduces variety, which in turn causes reality to be unclear, allowing for differing perspectives and interpretations of the same events. Viewing entrepreneurship as an emergent one recognises that entrepreneurship is not just about the individual - the risk-taking entrepreneur or leadership but about the environment, culture, and systems that enable new ideas and solutions to emerge. From this perspective, the entrepreneurship process is about navigating equivocal scenarios through iteration and improvisation. Accommodating equivocal situations has made the entrepreneurial journey a form of organisational evolution that blends constant change, improvisation, learning, adaptation, and the continuous challenging of assumptions, perceptions, and beliefs.

As a result of the evolutionary process, entrepreneurship becomes an emergent property because it arises from the interaction of various elements and conditions rather than being a result of any single factor. Venture creation aligns well with the broader idea of emergent properties in complex systems as it results from interactions of individuals, their environment and broader societal systems.

Viewing entrepreneurship as an emergent property emphasises:

1. Systemic and Collective Action: Entrepreneurship is something that emerges from networks of people, resources, and ideas. It is not only about the founder or leader but about the conditions that allow creativity and innovation to thrive collectively.
2. Dynamic Adaptability: This perspective acknowledges that entrepreneurship can evolve in response to changing market conditions, technology, and social needs, encouraging a more flexible and responsive approach to business and innovation.
3. Innovation Ecosystems: It shifts the focus from individual entrepreneurship to building ecosystems—where institutions, networks, and policies work together to create environments conducive to innovation and entrepreneurship. This view encourages collaboration, cross-pollination of ideas, and shared responsibility for growth and prosperity.
4. Breaking down Silos: This perspective helps break down traditional silos between different sectors, knowledge structures and actors, encouraging diversity and collaborations that address complex problems in innovative ways.

Understanding entrepreneurship as an emergent property shifts the focus from individual heroism to collective, system-driven innovation and entrepreneurship, creating a fertile ground for long-term, sustainable prosperity.

Organisational evolution leads to significant changes in the entity's nature compared to its initial state. Throughout the entrepreneurial process, the assumptions and values that support a sustainable venture often diverge considerably from those that originally inspired it. This evolution can also lead to modifications in products, services, and processes, which may diverge from initial plans.

Let's consider three organisations that have evolved significantly from their initial state:

1. Samsung: Samsung started in 1938 as a trading company selling groceries, dried fish, noodles, and other goods in South Korea. It later diversified into various sectors, including textiles, insurance, and retail. In the 1960s, Samsung entered the electronics market, initially producing black-and-white televisions. Over time, it expanded into a wide range of consumer electronics, including smartphones, semiconductors, and home appliances. Its rapid innovation in the mobile phone sector, from simple mobile handsets to flagship smartphones like the Galaxy series, dramatically shifted the company's identity. Samsung is now a global leader in technology and consumer electronics, with significant dominance in the semiconductor industry, display technology, and mobile communications. Its diversification into industries like shipbuilding, construction, and biopharmaceuticals has further strengthened its position as a major conglomerate.
2. Amazon: Originally launched in 1994 as an online bookstore, Amazon has evolved into a global e-commerce giant that offers a vast range of products, cloud computing services (AWS), streaming services, and even AI technology. Its shift from books to a diverse array of products and services and its growth into industries like cloud computing and logistics represents a significant departure from its initial business model.

3. Netflix: Netflix started in 1997 as a DVD rental service by mail, but over time, it evolved into a global leader in streaming entertainment. As digital streaming took over, Netflix pivoted from renting physical DVDs to offering online streaming of movies and TV shows. Eventually, the company expanded further into content production, becoming a major producer of original series and films, a complete departure from its original DVD-based service.
4. Microsoft: Microsoft evolved from a software company focused on operating systems to a global leader in cloud computing, AI, and enterprise solutions, shifting its focus from consumer software to services.

In all these cases, organisational evolution is clearly evident as products, services, and internal processes have far exceeded their initial visions, enabling the companies to remain relevant and competitive in dynamic industries. Organisational evolution integrates continuous change, improvisation, learning, adaptation, and the on-going challenge of assumptions, perceptions, and beliefs. All these changes required further adjustments to organisational routines, norms and structures to align with the changes in market conditions, technologies and consumer expectations.

This illustrates the core of entrepreneurship as an emergent property. The new organisation emerges from the tension between order and disorder, routine and creativity, predictability and chaos. It is a result of integrating the core elements of the business model in various ways until a viable solution emerges. This involves creating and modifying the entity's structure, acquiring and integrating resources, establishing a culture and implementing and adjusting processes and routines. The point here is that the resulting business entity undergoes continuous refinement through experimentation and adaptation, leading to the emergence of a more effective organisation. The emergent view implies that market-creating innovation and entrepreneurship further amplify environmental ambiguity and uncertainty by introducing new services and products where everything is constantly changing and regulating rules or guidelines are yet to be defined.

Dealing with Equivocal Situations

The need to promote prosperity challenges the traditional view of the entrepreneur by expanding the role of the entrepreneur beyond profit maximisation and risk-taking. Entrepreneurs are not just business creators but are agents of social, economic, and environmental change. While entrepreneurship has often been associated with starting businesses to generate wealth, the focus on promoting prosperity requires a broader perspective. Numerous studies have investigated what sets entrepreneurs apart from non-entrepreneurs. Early research uncovered the personal attributes and traits that enable entrepreneurs to identify and successfully exploit market opportunities that others overlook. This focus on simplistic personality traits, such as risk-taking, independence, problem-solving propensity, motivation, courage, and strong willpower, reinforced the notion that entrepreneurs are born, not made.

However, as entrepreneurs are becoming agents of social, economic, and environmental change rather than being business creators, this shift requires a new understanding of entrepreneurship. This new view of the entrepreneur emphasises long-term value creation, community impact and the development of sustainable solutions to social and economic problems. Entrepreneurs are individuals who identify opportunities for innovation and exploit them to drive broad-based prosperity, which involves not only creating wealth but also addressing systemic issues like poverty, inequality, and environmental sustainability.

Promoting prosperity challenges entrepreneurs to move beyond personal success and focus on collective well-being. It requires them to balance financial goals with social impact and responsibility, aligning their ventures with broader economic development objectives. This shift redefines entrepreneurship as a transformative force that shapes both markets and society, expanding our understanding of what makes the entrepreneur beyond individual traits and attributes.

Recent insights from cognitive psychology and behavioural sciences have highlighted the crucial role of mindsets and perspectives in innovation and entrepreneurship. This has led to the emergence of the cognitive perspective, which emphasises the entrepreneur's mental processes, behaviours and attitudes rather than personality traits. The cognitive approach considers the entrepreneur's knowledge structures, thought processes and experiences. By examining these elements, this approach has offered a deeper insight into how entrepreneurs successfully assess, judge and make decisions in equivocal situations throughout the entrepreneurial journey, distinguishing their decision-making processes from those of non-entrepreneurs.

The cognitive perspective emphasises that entrepreneurs are more diverse than alike, making it difficult to categorise them based on universal personality traits. Entrepreneurs come from all social backgrounds, each with unique beliefs, values, and personalities. It is now widely accepted that no one starts out as an inherent entrepreneur; rather, individuals become entrepreneurs by engaging in entrepreneurial activities. This view aligns with the emergent nature of entrepreneurship. Entrepreneurs are made from the dynamic environments in which the entrepreneurial process unfolds.

While an entrepreneur's personality attributes and traits are important, they alone are insufficient for successfully launching a new business. Human traits can change in response to external and internal stimuli. Culture, religion, education, work experience, and various demographic and environmental factors significantly influence entrepreneurial pursuits. Navigating equivocal situations requires leading with the right mindset and perspectives, which are crucial for effective management.

Research has demonstrated that successful entrepreneurs possess unique psychological attributes and cognitive abilities that allow them to process information and ideas differently, enabling them to identify market-creating opportunities that others overlook. These distinctive psychological traits and cognitive abilities can be distilled into three interrelated concepts, which form the foundation of the mindset and perspectives that distinguish entrepreneurs: entrepreneurial mindset, entrepreneurial alertness and absorptive capacity.

Let's explore each one of these concepts in detail.

Entrepreneurial Mindset

The entrepreneurial mindset is a way of thinking that embraces ambiguity, seizes opportunities and doesn't shy away from challenges. It consists of attitudes, values, and beliefs that empower individuals to sense and respond to uncertainty and ambiguity, paving the way for a new market and creating innovation. The entrepreneurial mindset relates to thought patterns and processes that shape the behaviour and attitudes of entrepreneurs. Mindset determines action. An entrepreneurial mindset encompasses a portfolio of skills and capabilities that includes autonomy, collaboration, creativity, critical thinking, problem-solving, flexibility, adaptability, tolerance for ambiguity and risk acceptance.

These competencies empower individuals and organisations to identify and capitalise on opportunities for market-creating innovation. They are essential not only for adapting to and managing change but also for shaping rapid transformations and uncertainties inherent in equivocal situations. An entrepreneurial mindset involves staying vigilant to and comprehending shifts that generate new market prospects, seizing these chances, and transforming them into thriving ventures.

While a few people are naturally inclined toward entrepreneurship, an entrepreneurial mindset is cultivated through deliberate practice and intentional effort. Some ways to develop this mindset include:

1. Embracing Failure: Embrace failure as an opportunity for learning and growth. Adopting a growth mindset, focused on continuous learning and improvement, is essential.
2. Think Creatively: Innovation is central to entrepreneurship. Cultivate creative thinking through activities such as brainstorming, ideation sessions, and engaging in creative hobbies.
3. Be Proactive: Take initiative and drive action. Act decisively without waiting for instructions, demonstrating proactive leadership.
4. Build a Strong Network: Establish relationships with like-minded individuals and seek mentors who provide guidance and support. A robust network of mentors, advisors, peers, and supporters is crucial for success.
5. Continuously Learn: Commit to lifelong learning. Stay current by reading, attending seminars, and pursuing learning opportunities to acquire new knowledge and skills for personal and professional growth.

Entrepreneurial Alertness

Entrepreneurial alertness involves vigilant observation and continuous monitoring of the environment to identify opportunities and other relevant market signals. Entrepreneurs have a heightened awareness of potential inaccuracies or gaps in one's knowledge, beliefs, assumptions or perceptions regarding market dynamics and their causal relationships. Success requires entrepreneurs to be prepared to encounter surprises and uncover new, pertinent information that may challenge their established assumptions, beliefs, and perceptions. Therefore, such alertness serves as a defence against cognitive biases such as functional fixedness and framing effects, which confines most individuals to rigid and singular interpretations of objects and information based on initial encounters. Overcoming these biases is essential for fostering creativity and innovation, thereby enhancing the potential for entrepreneurial success.

Entrepreneurial alertness entails a unique perspective and cognitive approach that enables entrepreneurs to identify opportunities even when not actively seeking them and envision future states once these opportunities are seized. This capability is crucial in making sense of market inconsistencies and reframing assumptions about market imperfections, a key process in uncovering entrepreneurial opportunities. Innovation hinges on making informed assumptions about markets or products because it sets the foundation for subsequent steps and activities in unlocking the identified opportunity.

Absorptive Capacity

Absorptive capacity, defined as the ability to learn, entails internalising new knowledge, integrating it with existing knowledge to create new knowledge and utilising it to innovate new capabilities, skills and products. In dynamic environments, successful entrepreneurship hinges significantly on the entrepreneur's capacity to swiftly absorb and apply knowledge. Identifying, developing, and seizing opportunities demands a robust foundation of business and technical acumen derived from prior education, professional experience, and on-going access to emerging knowledge. A deficiency in learning agility may prevent organisations and individuals from recognising pivotal knowledge and technological signals, resulting in missed opportunities to create new markets.

In the knowledge economy, market imbalances tend to vanish as quickly as they arise due to rapid technological progress. The imperative to comprehend emerging trends, adapt market perspectives and anticipate future conditions underscores the pivotal role of continuous learning in the entrepreneurial journey. Beyond the accumulation of knowledge, the ability to learn rapidly emerges as a cornerstone for success in navigating evolving market landscapes.

The relationship between entrepreneurial mindset, entrepreneurial alertness and absorptive capacity is a dynamic one, where each element complements and strengthens the others. An entrepreneurial mindset fosters the proactive attitude necessary for recognising and responding to emerging opportunities, a trait central to entrepreneurial alertness. The more developed the mindset, the sharper the ability to notice market gaps, trends, or innovations, allowing entrepreneurs to act on them.

Entrepreneurial alertness, in turn, feeds back into the mindset by reinforcing a constant search for opportunities, driving the entrepreneur to remain open, curious, and adaptable. This heightened awareness enables them to spot new ideas or challenges that require innovative solutions, which is crucial in a constantly changing environment. The absorptive capacity amplifies both by enabling entrepreneurs to absorb and integrate new knowledge into their decision-making processes.

With a strong absorptive capacity, entrepreneurs can not only identify opportunities but also effectively leverage external information, technologies, or insights to exploit them. This creates a feedback loop where alertness to new knowledge and trends is enriched by the capacity to understand, apply, and innovate with external inputs, making the entrepreneur more responsive, adaptive, and successful in seizing opportunities. Together, these factors drive continuous innovation and competitive advantage.

These three concepts shed light on how and why entrepreneurs are cognitively predisposed to identify and capitalise on opportunities that others overlook. They empower entrepreneurs to embrace ambiguity as an opportunity to learn, explore diverse options and experiment to generate innovative solutions. This enables them to skilfully navigate uncertain scenarios, establish routines and maintain stability amidst change by improvising and adapting to new developments and demands. These unique psychological traits and cognitive abilities support resilience, drive creativity and foster growth in modern, dynamic entrepreneurial environments. They are essential not only for identifying opportunities but also for ensuring success throughout the entrepreneurial process.

Mental Models

Africa's journey through underdevelopment is not unique in the context of global history. Regions such as the United States of America and China also endured significant periods of economic struggle and underdevelopment before transforming themselves into the global powerhouses they are today. In the 1800s, the average life expectancy in the US was just 45 years, with infant mortality rates as high as 200 deaths per 1,000 births, and fewer than 5% of the population had access to decent housing, clean water, and sanitation. The average person spends nearly all of their income on basic food needs, and government support is minimal, marred by widespread corruption and cronyism.

The US was once as impoverished as, if not more so than, many underdeveloped economies in Africa today. Its dramatic transformation from a struggling, underdeveloped nation to an economic powerhouse was neither a miracle nor an act of fate. It was driven by the powerful force that has uplifted many economies worldwide, including China and Singapore: innovation and entrepreneurship. The stories of these countries serve as powerful reminders that economic stagnation can be overcome with the right strategies, vision, and execution.

A compelling analogy exists in human behaviour: two individuals can face identical challenges, yet their outcomes can be vastly different—one may emerge resilient and successful, while the other is overwhelmed and defeated. What accounts for this stark difference?

The core lies in mental models. Mental models are the deeply ingrained beliefs, assumptions, and frameworks through which humans interpret the world and make decisions. These internal maps shape not only how individuals respond to challenges but also how entire societies approach opportunities and setbacks. In the cases of the US and China, their leaders and populations adopted innovative mental models that prioritised resilience, strategic investment, and long-term growth. For Africa, understanding and reconfiguring these mental frameworks is essential. To shift from surviving underdevelopment to promoting prosperity, there must be a transformation of our deeply ingrained assumptions, frameworks, stories or perspectives that shape how we understand the world, process information, and make decisions.

Developing the requisite entrepreneurial mindsets and perspectives demands more than just time and effort; it requires the adoption of new mental models. Mental models are internal representations of external realities that shape how we perceive and navigate the world. The challenge with mental models is not whether they are right or wrong but that most people remain unaware of their existence, and they often become out-dated. Operating subconsciously, these models influence our worldview, inform our understanding of how things work, and guide us in interpreting complex situations, both at work and in our personal lives. Consider navigating a city using a map created in 1980. Such a map would not reflect any changes that have occurred over the decades. Would you be able to find your favourite restaurant or sports club on that out-dated map? Likely not.

This analogy highlights the limitations of out-dated mental models. Just as an old map fails to guide us effectively in a modern city, out-dated mental models hinder our ability to interpret new experiences, solve current problems, and engage meaningfully with others. If mental models influence how we approach decision-making and problem-solving, how well can they serve us if they remain unchanged in today's fast-paced world? Will they effectively help us determine how we should interact with the world, make decisions and solve problems?

Altering mental models is quite challenging and even scary, as it requires changing our deeply ingrained assumptions, generalisations, and perceptions that have shaped our understanding of reality and guided our actions in the past. Yet, evidence around us clearly demonstrates that the mental maps that have served us thus far are insufficient to guide us into the future. As the landscape evolves, new mental frameworks become imperative. Emerging information, new experiences and insights, all point to the need to transform our internal representations of how the world operates and how we perceive and solve organisational problems.

To promote and support innovation and entrepreneurship within our businesses, communities and economies, we must embrace new ways of thinking and operating. There are four bedrock realities crucial for transforming our mental models as individuals. Adopting these four realities empowers an entrepreneurial mindset, enhances entrepreneurial alertness, and promotes the development of one's absorptive capacity.

The four bedrock realities of innovation and entrepreneurship are:

- The whole is greater than the sum of its parts
- Current conditions do not determine the future
- Leverage the wisdom of crowds
- Pursue value, technology is simply a great enabler

The Whole Is Greater Than the Sum of Its Parts

Popular leadership and management practices are deeply rooted in the principles of scientific management. Developed at the height of the Second Industrial Revolution, scientific management relied on deterministic, linear causal links. This perspective led to the design of public and private organisations governed by efficient cause-and-effect regulators. As we all learned in school, the management's primary roles are planning, organising, coordinating, and controlling. These roles are achieved by establishing and monitoring cause-and-effect rules and procedures for others to follow. Borrowed from engineering science, this mechanistic, linear thinking assumes that reality can be objectively understood through straightforward, linear causal relationships.

From this perspective, organisations are seen as machines composed of interconnected components. A company is the aggregate of its various departments, such as marketing, finance, and operations. Similarly, a family is the sum of its members—daughter, father, mother, son, cousin, and so on. From this understanding, problem-solving involves deconstructing the organisation into its constituent parts and critically analysing each component for faults or issues. Existing knowledge is deemed sufficient to define organisational problems and objectively determine the best course of action for resolution.

Such linear thinking and analysis were effective in traditional, simple environments where all existing information could be processed to develop the optimal course of action. However, the increasing complexity of today's context produces equivocal events characterised by surprise and shock. As previously mentioned, equivocal events create scenarios in which existing knowledge structures are inadequate for making sense of the world around us. Consequently, linear thinking falls significantly short in crafting effective strategies to respond to existing and emerging challenges.

Have you ever wondered why our best efforts aren't yielding the desired outcomes? Despite our clear intentions to improve things, our interventions often make the situation worse. Ambiguous events necessitate a shift from linear thinking to systems thinking. Without this shift, it is easy to blame external forces for our problems and play the victim. Victim mentality and the associated tendency to shift blame has been one of Africa's biggest challenges.

As I write this, South Africa is approaching general elections, and the current president, Cyril Ramaphosa, is making news headlines, blaming the colonial regime for the country's current problems. Yet, it has been 30 years since South Africa attained political freedom and has been hailed as a modern democracy. Fault-finding and blame games are prevalent in many economies, homes and workplaces, but they are signs of weakness. Engaging in them diminishes our power and capacity to control our destiny. We neglect personal agency and responsibility in contributing to the creation of those circumstances for which we blame others. Children blame parents for their behaviour, the marketing team blames operations for missing sales targets, and operations blame the finance department.

Africa effectively leverages its existing knowledge and resources to develop home-grown solutions that empower organisations and communities to address the root causes of poverty and underdevelopment. This requires thinking in terms of systems instead of parts to enable and support the development of sustainable, holistic strategies that prioritise community empowerment and tackle the multifaceted nature of poverty and underdevelopment.

In addressing the complex challenges faced by modern organisations and communities, linear thinking tends to oversimplify problem-solving by assuming objectivity and rationality. However, our perception of reality is inherently subjective, shaped by mental frameworks and shared beliefs. The pursuit of pure objectivity and rational decision-making often leads to an illusion of control, resulting in a limited understanding of the issues we aim to resolve and the implementation of ineffective, short-term solutions. This approach not only restricts our problem-solving capabilities but also stifles creativity and innovation, preventing the development of sustainable strategies that align with the dynamic nature of contemporary challenges. Embracing a more nuanced and adaptive way of thinking is essential for promoting prosperity and resilience.

Discovering and realising market creation and innovation opportunities necessitate a paradigm shift. Shifting from viewing the organisation as a mere collection of parts to perceiving it as a unified entity is greater than the sum of its parts. This is the essence of systems thinking. Systems thinking entails perceiving an organisation as an interconnected whole or unit. It provides a holistic view in which an organisation comprises interdependent parts that themselves form integrated wholes. It transcends the simple mechanistic structures, embodying a complex and evolving entity composed of nested systems within larger systems.

For example, within a business (which is a system), departments function as subsystems, which in turn may consist of teams (sub-subsystems). The firm itself operates within an industry, which is another system, and the industry is a part of the broader economy—a larger system. Similarly, a family operates as a system composed of individuals (subsystems) who are both autonomous and interdependent, participating in other systems such as schools, workplaces, social clubs and communities.

In essence, a system is an integrated whole pursuing its defined purposes and objectives. In managing such systems, the focus of leadership lies in aligning the goals and objectives of subsystems with the broader purpose of the overarching system.

The behaviour of an organisation is intricately shaped by the interconnectivity, interrelationships, and interactions among its components. Each constituent part not only influences but is also influenced by other parts, creating reciprocal effects that extend both internally and externally. The extent of influence wielded by each component in driving significant organisational transformation or change depends on the organisational structure and its operational dynamics as a cohesive entity. The concept of systems thinking emphasises that within any system, whether a business, family, or industry, various interconnected parts work together, influencing and being influenced by one another. This interconnectedness means that change in one part of the system can trigger changes in others, impacting the whole. Effective leadership requires understanding these relationships and aligning the objectives of individual parts (subsystems) with the overarching goals of the entire system.

For example, consider a car as a system. The engine, brakes, transmission, and wheels are subsystems that must function well individually, but their true effectiveness lies in how they work together. If the brakes (a subsystem) fail, the entire car's safety and performance are compromised. Similarly, improving one part, like adding a more powerful engine, only benefits the car if other parts, such as the transmission, are adapted to handle the increased power. This illustrates how interconnected components shape the overall behaviour and effectiveness of the system as a whole.

It is vital to recognise and understand how the behaviour of each component of an organisation influences and is influenced by the behaviour of others, both within and outside the organisation, in addressing our most pressing challenges. This reality offers a comprehensive way of thinking and approaching organisational issues and provides a platform for exploration and experimentation rather than linear thinking. Systems thinking is indispensable for fostering innovation as it fundamentally enhances awareness of the following aspects:

1. The interdependencies and relationships among the organisation's interacting parts and its external partners or stakeholders are often non-linear rather than linear. Non-linear interactions can amplify small changes to produce disproportionately large effects.
2. It recognises that organisations demonstrate emergent properties, which may lead to unintended consequences from well-intentioned actions. Emergent properties encompass both positive and negative characteristics or behaviours that arise from the interdependent interactions among the organisation's internal and external components.

Awareness of these two aspects is profound and transformative. It allows us to recognise our responsibility as individuals and organisations in shaping the social and economic challenges we intend to understand and resolve. Rather than being mere pieces on a chessboard constrained by external rules and dynamics, we possess the power to both influence and be influenced by our environment. It empowers us to redesign the chessboard, establish new rules, or even create an entirely new game with a totally different structure to enable new patterns, rules, connections and modes of interaction or behaviour. This is at the heart of innovation and entrepreneurship.

Entrepreneurship is rooted in the conviction that reality is socially constructed. With this belief, we actively seek plausible interpretations of the world by adjusting our knowledge structures, recognising and making sense of the equivocal events and ultimately coordinating responses that allow for tentative action despite uncertainty and imperfection.

In a world of increasing complexity, systems thinking aids entrepreneurship by providing the following:

1. *Creating Order out of Chaos*

The idea of "creating order amid chaos" refers to the ability to bring clarity and structure to complex situations by understanding how various elements interact within a system. We are confronted with complex problems influenced by multiple interconnected factors. Adopting a systems perspective offers a robust framework for managing this complexity. By mapping relationships and interdependencies among parts and systems, entrepreneurs and leaders can understand interactions and see the big picture, encompassing various stakeholders, market forces, and internal processes. This holistic view creates clarity, enabling the identification of key areas and leverage points where small changes can significantly impact the entire system. It also aids in prioritising efforts and resources more effectively, focusing on areas that will yield the greatest results. In a world of increasing complexity, especially for entrepreneurs, this approach helps navigate challenges by identifying key areas where small changes can lead to significant improvements.

Imagine a small manufacturing business struggling with frequent supply chain disruptions, customer complaints, and low employee morale. Each of these issues seems separate and overwhelming on its own. However, by adopting a systems thinking approach, the business owner maps out how the supply chain, customer feedback, and internal team dynamics are interconnected. Upon analysing the relationships, the owner realises that improving communication between the sales team and suppliers could prevent delays, reduce customer complaints, and boost employee morale due to smoother operations. By focusing on this one leverage point—communication—the business owner creates order and efficiency amid what initially seemed like a chaotic situation. This holistic view allows the entrepreneur to prioritise actions that would have the greatest positive impact on the business as a whole.

2. *Capacity to Anticipate Unintended and Intended Consequences of Interventions*

By adopting a systems perspective, entrepreneurs gain insight into how their decisions can create reinforcing loops that drive desired outcomes or balancing loops that generate counteracting effects, potentially leading to unexpected results. Recognising these feedback mechanisms enables entrepreneurs to foresee the ripple effects—both positive and negative—of their actions within a system over time. This understanding allows for more informed decision-making, as entrepreneurs can anticipate the broader impact of their choices. The ability to anticipate consequences is crucial for learning, adapting, and seizing growth opportunities while also helping avoid unintended outcomes and ensuring effective resource allocation. Ultimately, this approach fosters long-term success and strengthens organisational resilience. Consider a company that has decided to implement a new sales incentive program to increase performance. The intended consequence is a boost in sales as employees work harder to earn the rewards. However, this action can result in unintended consequences. Some employees are prioritising sales volume over customer satisfaction to maximise their bonuses, causing harm to the company's reputation and leading to customer loss.

By recognising this balancing loop, the management can adjust the program to ensure that incentives align with both sales and customer satisfaction, ensuring that the intervention leads to the intended result without negative side effects.

3. *Promoting Shared Responsibility and Collaboration*

Systems thinking emphasises the interconnectedness of actions and consequences, highlighting the interdependence within organisations and communities. It encourages both individuals and organisations to consider the broader impact of their actions and take collective responsibility. This shared responsibility fosters collaboration and collective problem-solving, integrating diverse perspectives and expertise to develop more effective strategies for addressing systemic challenges.

Without a strong sense of responsibility, building a culture of collaboration among stakeholders is challenging. Problems are viewed in isolation, leading to blame-shifting rather than sustainable solutions. Recognising interdependence and understanding how individual choices affect others within the system taps into human empathy and compassion, promoting inclusion and diversity. This approach fosters a more holistic understanding of challenges and encourages collaborative efforts to address them.

By incorporating diverse perspectives into problem-solving, stakeholders can create a shared understanding and co-develop solutions that reflect the needs and concerns of all parties. Collaboration across departments, disciplines, industries, or even nations allows entrepreneurs to leverage a wide range of insights and skills, resulting in more effective solutions to complex problems.

4. *Learning and Adaptation*

In today's complex and dynamic business environment, adaptability is essential for success. By adopting a systems perspective in problem-solving, individuals understand that solutions are not static but require continuous refinement as new information surfaces or the system evolves. This mindset nurtures a culture of on-going improvement and learning, where individuals stay open to feedback, experimentation, and adaptation. Collaboration plays a crucial role in this process, enabling diverse stakeholders to share insights and observations, which in turn facilitate collective learning and effective problem-solving.

The systems perspective offers innovators and entrepreneurs a transformative lens to navigate the ever-changing organisational landscape. By examining the intricate relationships and interactions within the organisation, they can better identify and address challenges, paving the way for the emergence of new, beneficial patterns. This approach increases the likelihood of crafting innovative solutions that drive exponential growth and prosperity. Recognising the interconnected nature of systems, rather than adhering to linear progressions, is key to seeing reality in a way that empowers transformative change.

Current Conditions Do Not Determine the Future

The corporate world is still relying on industrial-era strategic management tools and theories that emphasise stability, predictability and adherence to predefined processes and roles. Designed to create near-perfect market conditions by reducing uncertainty and providing an illusion of control, these tools and theories analyse current market conditions to inform potential future outcomes. This approach is grounded in the belief that by understanding the present, we can model how the future may evolve. Decision-making and goal-setting are based on existing data, trends, and assumptions about how the future will unfold. By projecting the present into the future, leaders create a well-defined path forward, which provides a false of control and presumed certainty.

For example, a business leader might use current sales data, market conditions, and customer behaviour patterns to project future outcomes. By projecting these conditions into the future, they can create structured strategies and set clear milestones for achieving future success. The risk is that this approach overly relies on the assumption that the present conditions will continue as expected, i.e., the structure will remain the same. This approach has led to what is known as leading by structure, managing and making decisions within the boundaries of what is currently known and established.

While leading with structure was effective during the stable and predictable industrial era, it is less suited for today's dynamic and complex environment. The rapid pace of change means assumptions can quickly become out-dated, demanding that leaders adopt more agile and adaptable strategies. Relying solely on structured approaches limits flexibility and hinders the ability to respond effectively when unexpected challenges arise.

Assuming current market conditions will remain unchanged, hindering innovation and entrepreneurship. This mindset limits the scope of what is seen as possible, profitable, and sustainable, confining strategic thinking to present-day realities. While strategic plans should acknowledge market realities and align with current resources, industry standards, and best practices, overly focusing on these aspects binds organisations to the status quo. Conventional business theory calls this alignment with existing market conditions "strategic fit," which shifts management's focus from pursuing long-term growth and prosperity to prioritising short-term goals like meeting budgets, achieving quarterly earnings, and paying bills. Such an approach restricts creative thinking and innovation, as it prioritises immediate stability over exploring new opportunities that could drive future success.

To foster a culture of entrepreneurship and innovation, leaders must embrace uncertainty and invest in long-term potential. Market-creating innovations do not strategically fit current market realities, industry standards and best practices. Nokia lost its dominant market position in the mobile phones sector to Samsung and Apple who did not respect industry standards and best practices. Market-creating innovation does not align with short-term goals such as shareholder value or quarterly earnings per share. Amazon and Uber operated for more than five years without reporting any operating profit, yet today, they are shining jewels.

Discovering and unlocking market creating innovations requires us to lead with agency instead of structure. Leading with agency begins in the mind, envisioning what could be and should be, regardless of the current reality. It involves tapping into the power of independent thinking and self-direction, inspiring initiative rather than waiting for circumstances to dictate actions. It prioritises making informed decisions based on purpose, vision and values rather than solely relying on external inputs. Individuals and organisations that lead with agency set clear goals to create the future they imagine and desire and align their actions to achieve these goals by anticipating challenges and opportunities.

Leading with structure comes from understanding that current conditions do not determine future possibilities. The interplay of human ingenuity and the impact of environmental constraints create a future that is totally different from existing conditions. Innovators do not uncover market-creating innovations by adhering to existing rules or industry standards. Henry Ford wisely captured this insight when he remarked that if he had asked people what they wanted, they would have said a faster horse instead of a car.

Market-creating innovations emerge from individuals and organisations that recognise the sovereignty of their minds, harness the power of imagination and possess the capacity to reimagine and create the world they envision. These individuals challenge current market conditions to create what could be. They boldly ask the right questions, allowing them to see opportunities others miss and to envision what is possible and how to achieve it. They do not waste time and energy imagining why something won't work or cannot be done; instead, they ask, "Why not?" and "What if?"

Leading with the agency is not only uncommon but also difficult to advocate for. Focusing on the immediate environment seems very reasonable, but it diverts individuals and organisations from their greatest strengths: imagination and the power of choice to transcend the current circumstances to create new realities. In schools, we have all been conditioned to gravitate towards what can be easily measured rather than explore what is possible. Entrepreneurs lead with the agency. They know that what is merely reasonable does not result in market-creating innovations.

Leverage the Wisdom of Crowds

Many of us have been conditioned to believe that valuable knowledge resides exclusively within the minds of a privileged few. This mind set is prevalent in the corporate world as well, where the key to solving organisational problems or making good decisions is to find that one person with the right answer. Have you ever wondered why digital-era entrepreneurs have risen to celebrity status? It is because earlier views on innovation focused on the entrepreneur's creativity, boldness and gut instincts as the drivers of market-creating innovations and growth. Schumpeter famously depicted the entrepreneur as a rare and scarce resource to be treasured. An entrepreneur was seen as the guy with the answers.

While recognising the significant contributions of founders, this almost mystical reverence for entrepreneurs has become deeply ingrained in our minds, creating a cognitive barrier that prevents many of us from appreciating our inborn creativity capabilities. This mindset restricts our perspectives on innovation and creativity. Remember, perspective is everything.

Elevating the gifted and instinctive entrepreneur overshadows the creativity and contributions of others. This phenomenon is evident in the contemporary music industry, where the lead singer often draws the spotlight when music is actually co-created by the band. In reality, entrepreneurship resembles an orchestra than a soloist; a diverse group is far better equipped to make decisions that impact the lives of many than an isolated individual.

While not everyone is equally creative, most of us possess enough creativity to significantly contribute to collective problem-solving. Attributes like creativity, humour, style and initiative are not reserved for a privileged few but are found among many. Creating something entirely new is extremely challenging; the path to full realisation is uncertain; it's a dive into the unknown. Harnessing the power of diverse perspectives, along with an appreciation for others' ingenuity, enhances the likelihood of success. A rich tapestry of human creativity and ideas is essential for addressing our most pressing challenges.

In his book *The Wisdom of Crowds,* James Surowiecki outlines three types of problems where collective wisdom can surpass the expertise of a few individuals, given the right group dynamics:

1. Cognition Problems: These are issues with clear solutions or optimal answers. Examples include predicting sports outcomes, forecasting sales, and

assessing the likelihood of regulatory approvals. Determining the best location for a public facility also falls within this category.

2. Coordination Problems: These require individuals to synchronise or align their behaviours with others in the group. Examples include establishing fair trade prices, organising company operations, and navigating safely in heavy traffic.
3. Cooperation Problems: These problems involve motivating self-interested individuals to collaborate despite potential conflicts of interest. Examples include paying taxes, tackling pollution, and reaching agreements on fair compensation.

The focus of this book does not extend to exploring these specific sets of problems. However, it is essential to understand that the entrepreneurship process – transforming a market-creating innovation from an idea into a viable business – is more than a solo act. It demands a diverse network of people with varied perspectives and skills to collaborate effectively. This process entails addressing on-going challenges related to cognition, coordination and cooperation.

Throughout history, the business and economic landscape has been shaped by both visionary entrepreneurs and the collective wisdom of carefully selected individuals rather than a random crowd. These talented individuals possess the ability to identify what must be learned or unlearned, comprehensively evaluate relevant factors, and integrate them to develop sustainable and innovative solutions to complex problems.

To effectively leverage the wisdom of crowds, there are five essential group dynamics that play a crucial role in ensuring the success of collaborative efforts in entrepreneurship and innovation:

1. *Diversity of Participants*

A diverse group brings different perspectives, expertise, and experiences, which is key to generating innovative solutions. Diversity fosters creativity by ensuring that ideas come from various viewpoints and backgrounds. Without diversity, a group risks missing out on unique insights that can lead to breakthrough ideas. To ensure this, it is important to include individuals from various fields, cultures, and levels of experience, creating a richer pool of ideas.

2. *Decentralisation of Influence*

Effective crowdsourcing relies on the decentralisation of influence, meaning no single voice or subgroup should dominate the conversation. When participants are free from the constraints of hierarchical or dominant voices, the group benefits from the full range of ideas. To encourage this, platforms or methods that anonymise contributions or enable equal participation can prevent power dynamics from skewing the process and ensure a fair exchange of ideas.

3. *Clear Objectives and Purpose*

A well-defined goal or problem is essential for effective group dynamics. Without a clear understanding of the objective, efforts become scattered and unfocused. When participants know exactly what they are trying to achieve, they contribute more relevant and actionable insights. Clear goals direct the flow of the conversation, keeping the group focused on solving the problem at hand rather than veering off course.

4. *Psychological Safety and Open Communication*

Creating an environment where participants feel safe to share their ideas without fear of judgment is fundamental. Psychological safety encourages open communication and fosters an atmosphere of trust. When people feel their contributions are valued and respected, they are more likely to speak up, leading to a more robust exchange of ideas and more innovative solutions. To ensure psychological safety, it is important to build a culture of constructive feedback and respect.

5. *Independent Thinking*

For crowdsourcing to generate optimal results, participants must be able to think independently. Independent thinking prevents conformity, encourages unique perspectives, and ensures that solutions are not limited by the dominant opinions within the group. When individuals contribute their original thoughts without undue influence, the crowd's collective intelligence can lead to more innovative outcomes. This approach is particularly useful in problem-solving, as diverse and original input fosters more creative and effective solutions.

Pursue Value, Technology Is Simply a Great Enabler

To many, the word innovation is synonymous with technology innovation. The hype surrounding technology innovation makes it easy to become seduced by technology. Media, investors, and tech enthusiasts have been hyping up the transformative potential of digital technologies, leading to a belief that they hold the key to breakthrough innovation. This can lead to an over-reliance on technology as a solution to problems that may require deeper, non-tech-driven insights.

While technology is a tool used to create value, it is not an end in itself. A great piece of technology may not succeed in the market if it does not solve a clear problem or meet a real need. Technology serves as a powerful enabler of market-creating innovation, but markets respond to the value delivered, not the technology used. It is a superior value that inspires market demand and drives revenues and profits at the firm level. New markets emerge only from innovations that offer unprecedented value to users or customers.

In their book *Blue Ocean Strategy,* W. Chan Kim and Renée Mauborgne define value innovation as an innovation that provides buyers with a leap in value, creating value in real use. Value innovation arises from the simultaneous pursuit of differentiation and low cost, resulting in a leap in value for both the company and its customers. It creates new markets by developing and introducing unique features that distinguish a product or service from existing offerings at relatively lower costs. To create new markets, focus on identifying factors that create and deliver superior value first, then leverage technology to enable it. This approach ensures the commercial success of market-creating innovations and a strong return on investment.

In market-creating innovation, competition is never a benchmark but can make it irrelevant by creating a leap in value for both buyers and your organisation. Consequently, prioritising creating new compelling value for users serves as a critical guide for innovators, keeping their focus on achieving real-world use. Many tech innovations — like the Segway or Google Glass — were technologically advanced but did not create enough perceived value to capture significant market adoption. A well-known example of the importance of value innovation is the case of Xerox PARC. Despite developing numerous technological advancements, including the graphical user interface (GUI), Xerox PARC failed to commercialise these innovations successfully. The GUI, now common in all smartphones and computers, was first adopted from Xerox PARC by Steve Jobs. Recognising its potential, Jobs integrated it into a simple and intuitive interface for Apple's personal computers, which later evolved into iOS for mobile devices. It was Apple's ingenuity and creativity that transformed Xerox PARC's technology innovation into a market-creating innovation.

A Paradigm Shift

A paradigm shift is essential to fundamentally transform our approach to addressing our social and economic challenges, from alleviating poverty to creating prosperity. These four realities serve as critical success factors, and embracing them opens the minds of public and private sector leaders and entrepreneurs, making them perceptive to market-creating opportunities. They shape conversations, perceptions and attitudes, inspiring a culture of creativity that is so fundamental to new market creation. If a significant number of our leaders, students, and knowledge workers adopt these new insights and reshape their mental models, Africa can experience the transformative paradigm shift needed to change the continent's economic fortunes.

Equipped with the right perspectives, let's explore the two pathways to market-creating innovation in the next chapter.

Chapter 4

Pathways to Market-creating Innovation

In the previous section, we emphasized the importance of entrepreneurial mindsets and perspectives in driving entrepreneurship and innovation. However, without intention, these perspectives lack substance. Intention extends beyond mere desire or interest; it represents the strategic commitment and readiness to take action. It is the deliberate, goal-oriented mindset that guides actions, fuels perseverance, and anchors strategic decision-making. It lays the groundwork for transforming ideas into reality and serves as a powerful predictor of entrepreneurial success.

We all recognize the fundamental principle of cause and effect: every action triggers a reaction, and every outcome can be traced back to its source. Intention serves as the mental foundation for action, acting as the precursor in the cause-and-effect dynamic. This principle holds as true for innovation and entrepreneurship as it does for any other facet of life. New markets are not discovered; they are deliberately created through strategic and intentional innovation. When we have a clear, strong intention to build new markets, it becomes the driving force behind purposeful actions. These actions, when executed thoughtfully, set off a series of events that produce the desired outcomes. In essence, intention is what sets the cause in motion.

Understanding the interplay between intention and the law of cause and effect reveals that market-creating innovation stems from deliberate managerial action and strategy. However, operating with intention requires clarity on which actions lead to specific outcomes. This insight helps direct efforts and resources toward activities that achieve desired results. This is where shared vision comes into play as a critical part of this dynamic.

Intention without vision leads to aimless, unfocused effort. It is not uncommon for leaders to take action for action's sake without a clear goal in sight. While this may sound irrational, it happens frequently, resulting in misaligned strategies and wasted resources. Conversely, vision without intention is like having a roadmap and a destination but no vehicle to get you there. While the vision may be inspiring, it remains a wish unless supported by deliberate, goal-oriented action.

Without intention, leaders and entrepreneurs will surely struggle to turn their vision into reality, resulting in frustration and stagnation. However, when vision and intention are aligned, they form a powerful combination. Vision defines the *why*, while intention clarifies the *how*. Both must be communicated clearly. Effectively sharing both vision and intention with team members fosters alignment, motivation, and collective action towards market-creating innovation. It promotes ownership and encourages the entire team or organization to engage in meaningful conversations about driving innovation that shapes new markets.

This section discusses the overarching pathways to market-creating innovation: disruptive and non-disruptive. The goal is not to help you choose the best pathway because there is no "best" pathway. The path you take to creating a new market is determined by the nature of the problem you intend to solve. Therefore, this chapter aims to equip entrepreneurs and business leaders to approach their market-creating innovation with clear intentions and a stronger understanding of the types of outcomes they seek. This understanding guides strategic decisions and choices, such as areas to invest in, partnerships to establish and technologies to adopt. Each of these should be an intentional action designed to drive market innovation and secure a competitive advantage.

This objective shall be achieved by developing a comprehensive understanding of the problem you aim to address and recognizing its underlying nature. It shall be accomplished in two ways:

- First, by thoroughly examining the two pathways to market-creating innovation and
- Second, by purposefully evaluating the key elements of each pathway.

The Disruptive Pathway

This is a pathway to creating a new market in the existing industry by providing a solution that offers buyers or users a leap in value that is far greater than the existing solutions. Commonly known as disruptive innovation, it refers to innovations that create new markets by introducing simpler, more affordable products or services that initially appeal to a niche segment, which is often overlooked by mainstream players. Over time, these innovations improve, eventually disrupting established market leaders and reshaping industries.

The disruptive pathway creates a new market at the cost of the old one. Disruptive innovation offers a different value proposition that serves a previously unmet or underserved need. This challenges the status quo and opens opportunities for new customers and business models, leading to the displacement of older, established competitors. The industry to be disrupted provides a known target market size with a known need for which targeted customers have demonstrated a willingness to pay.

It is creating a new market inside an existing industry boundary by disrupting and displacing existing companies and jobs. As a result, economic growth comes with the social cost of displacement. Disruptive innovation as a concept was popularised by Clayton Christensen (1997) in his seminal work, *The Innovator's Dilemma*. Although the term was coined by Christensen, it builds on Joseph Schumpeter's earlier ideas of "creative destruction", introduced in 1942. Schumpeter observed that saturated markets experience diminishing returns, and true economic growth and prosperity can only emerge from market-creating innovations that replace existing processes, products, and services.

"Disruption" describes a process whereby a smaller, new entrant competitor with limited resources is able to successfully challenge an established incumbent business. Disruptive innovations are not breakthrough technologies that make existing market offerings better; rather, they are innovations that make products and services more accessible or provide convenience at affordable prices, thereby making them available and appealing initially to a less demanding but larger customer base than existing market solutions. It begins with products or services that take root in simple applications at the lower end of a market. Over time, these innovations improve in quality and capability, allowing delivery of greater consumer surplus and eventually moving upmarket from the fringes (the low end of the market or a new market) to the mainstream eroding first the incumbents' market share and then their profitability. This process is characterised by several key features:

- Creating an Initial Perception of Inferiority: Typically, these innovations begin with lower performance dimensions than existing products but target underserved or non-consumers—individuals who cannot afford or have limited access to traditional solutions. By effectively catering to these overlooked segments, these innovations slowly establish a foothold without directly challenging incumbent companies. Incumbent customers often perceive these offerings as inferior and are unlikely to switch, as they don't find them appealing. As a result, incumbent management tends to overlook the emerging threat, focusing instead on the needs of their mainstream customers.

- Market Penetration: Disruptive innovations often begin as simpler or lower-quality versions of existing products, providing just enough value to attract a specific group of customers. Over time, these innovations improve, eventually becoming competitive with or even superior to incumbents' offerings by delivering suitable functionality at a lower price. The objective is not to carve out a unique niche within the existing market but to establish a strong foundation for a broader competitive assault. While incumbents focus on enhancing their products and services for their most demanding and profitable customers, disruptors can differentiate their offerings by continuously making incremental improvements while simultaneously building layers of advantages. By adopting novel approaches that significantly lower the cost structure, they can achieve both differentiation and cost leadership.
- Upmarket Movement: As these innovations evolve, they begin to offer greater value at the same price, gradually attracting the mainstream customers of incumbents. While retaining the features that contributed to their initial success, these innovations shift the competitive landscape, putting incumbents at a disadvantage. Over time, customers move away from established offerings, increasingly adopting new products. By the time incumbents recognise the threat, it is often too late to defend their market share and profits.

The ultimate goal of disruptive innovation is not merely to imitate incumbents but also to outpace them through innovation, disrupting and displacing them. Disruptive innovations transform industries by creating new market leaders, redefining customer expectations, and frequently rendering established players obsolete.

To deliberately enable and successfully achieve disruptive innovation consider the following strategies:

1. *Business Model Innovation*

Business model innovation is indeed a vital component of disruptive innovation. While disruptive innovation typically focuses on creating new products or services that challenge existing market leaders, business model innovation provides the framework for how these products or services are delivered, priced, and consumed. It is this shift in the business model that often allows disruptive innovations to scale, attract mainstream customers, and ultimately displace incumbents in the following ways:

- *Targets Non-consumers*: Developing a business model that targets delivering value to those who have never purchased or used industry products and low-end consumers and who are the least profitable customers is crucial for the growth of disruptive innovations. The emphasis should be on perfecting the business model rather than just the product itself, as this helps define the unique value proposition and cost structure. Business model innovation often reshapes the value proposition to enhance accessibility, affordability, and convenience. For instance, companies like Uber and Airbnb disrupted traditional industries not only by introducing new services but also by reimagining how those services were delivered and monetised. Uber changed the way people access transportation, while Airbnb transformed how people find accommodation.
- *Changing Engagement Rules:* A significant aspect of business model innovation within disruption is its

ability to transform customer and supplier engagement. A well-designed business model redefines how businesses interact with the market, enabling a rapid shift from niche adoption to mainstream acceptance. Successful disruptive innovators often bypass traditional intermediaries, opting for direct interactions with customers and suppliers. They leverage digital channels to deliver services that are more personalised, efficient, and transparent. For example, Tesla revolutionised the automotive industry not just with electric vehicles but by altering customer engagement through a direct-to-consumer sales model, bypassing conventional dealerships.

Changing the rules of engagement lowers barriers to entry for newcomers, making it easier to compete with established players.

- *Creating New Revenue Streams and Pricing Models:* Disruptive innovation often relies on new revenue models that established players may overlook. For instance, the shift from ownership to access—illustrated by car-sharing services and streaming platforms—is a fundamental aspect of business model innovation that drives disruption. By adopting innovative pricing strategies such as pay-per-use or subscription models and leveraging technology to optimise distribution, new market entrants can offer products or services at lower costs or with added value. This approach enables them to attract underserved segments of the market. These models not only deliver value to customers in novel ways but also introduce alternative revenue streams that incumbents are typically slow to embrace. A prime example is Netflix, which transformed the video rental industry by pioneering a subscription-based streaming service that provided consistent, recurring revenue while changing how people consumed content.

Business model innovation allows new entrants to offer compelling alternatives that better align with customer needs, often in ways that incumbents struggle to respond to.

2. *Embrace and Adopt Enabling Technology*

Leveraging technology is a critical success factor in achieving disruptive innovation as it enables new entrants to overcome traditional barriers and deliver superior value. Leveraging leading-edge technology enables disruptive innovation to deliver new value at scale. Focus on technologies that make offerings more affordable and accessible to a broader audience. By improving accessibility and affordability, technology helps disruptors target underserved or non-consumer markets, offering products and services at lower costs or with added value.

Additionally, it streamlines operations and distribution, allowing businesses to scale rapidly while maintaining efficiency, which incumbents with legacy systems often cannot match. Technology facilitates the creation of innovative business models, such as subscription services or platform ecosystems, which generate consistent revenue streams and enhance customer and employee engagement. These models are often difficult for established players to replicate.

Moreover, data-driven insights allow disruptors to personalise offerings and improve customer experiences, giving them an edge over competitors who rely on traditional methods.

Digital technologies are lowering the cost of entry, empowering start-ups to compete with larger companies by leveraging cloud-based tools and other digital platforms. On the other hand, artificial intelligence is facilitating the creation of platform-based businesses that benefit from network and learning effects, where the value of a service grows as more people use it, accelerating expansion.

However, while technology is a powerful enabler, it is not the defining feature of disruptive innovation, even in technology-driven industries. Many business models and processes were established long before digital technology became widespread. The key lies in using technology as a catalyst for business model innovation, enhancing accessibility, scalability, and efficiency while maintaining a focus on addressing unmet market needs.

3. *Build a Coherent Value Network*

A value network consists of interconnected businesses, suppliers, customers, and other stakeholders that work together to create and deliver value. Through these partnerships, businesses can pool resources, share knowledge, and leverage each other's strengths, accelerating innovation and reducing costs. This collaboration helps new entrants scale faster and compete with larger incumbents.

Network effects are a key benefit of a value network. As more users, suppliers, or service providers join the network, its value increases, creating a competitive advantage. This is especially important for platform businesses, where each new participant strengthens the ecosystem. A strong value network also boosts adaptability and resilience, enabling businesses to quickly respond to market changes or technological shifts by accessing a broad range of resources and expertise.

A value network provides access to new markets and customer segments by leveraging partners' existing relationships and distribution channels. This helps disruptors expand faster and reach previously untapped audiences. Overall, building a value network accelerates innovation, enhances scalability and provides a sustainable competitive edge to tackle incumbents, making it a key factor in achieving success through disruptive innovation.

Sources of Disruptive Opportunities

Identifying disruptive opportunities starts with idea generation, but an idea is not synonymous with an opportunity. Ideas are everywhere, but there is a need for good sources of ideas that can be developed into market-creating opportunities. Entrepreneurial opportunities reside in existing but unexplored problems and in emerging problems due to changes or shifts in economic, social and technological factors. Solving these problems with a solution that is within the existing industry boundary creates a disruptive innovation. Peter Drucker suggested two good sources of generating ideas for disruptive opportunities.

1. *Anticipating Industry Future Developments*

Anticipating future developments that are already in motion in an industry provides disruptive opportunities. Changes in technology, demographics, societal perceptions and industry structures offer promising opportunities for industry re-creation and expansion. Whenever there are shifts in the economy or society, a delay typically occurs between the onset of change and its widespread effects. This lag time presents the potential for disruptive creations.

Amazon managed to disrupt the retail industry because Jeff Bezos anticipated and capitalised on the internet and related digital technological developments. Although there was a strong belief that these technologies would have a massive impact, it was difficult to foresee the specifics. Anticipating future industry development requires looking at other industries, other countries and other markets to assess whether anything has happened there that might establish a pattern in your industry, country or market.

2. *Making the Future Happen*

New ideas, knowledge, perceptions or technologies expected to shape the future of an industry over the next probably five to ten years come with massive disruptive opportunities. While these new ideas, knowledge, perceptions or technologies might not be immediately transformative, they are predicted to have a higher potential to create a future vastly different from today. This is exemplified by the founding of Econet, the telecommunications company. Strive Masiyiwa recognised the potential of mobile communication and digital networks long before they became mainstream and diligently worked to bring his vision to fruition.

Recognising the hidden disruptive potential of new ideas, perceptions, or technologies begins with embracing a vision of a different economy or society. Making the future happen requires questioning and overturning deeply entrenched economic or market assumptions and current industry practices and habits. Disruptive opportunities of this nature demand a commitment to transforming entire systems or organisations, not just modifying existing structures. While most people focus on the immediate present and struggle to envision future possibilities, taking deliberate and proactive steps toward creating this vision a reality is essential.

A Necessary Evil

Well-managed companies, adhering to best practices, struggle to respond to disruptive innovations and face their eternal demise. Their internal capabilities, organisational structures, and decision-making processes designed to sustain existing operations make them vulnerable to disruptive competitors. This has led to disruptive innovation being heavily criticised for unleashing very real negative effects on the economy and society. We have witnessed workers being made redundant, plants and equipment becoming obsolete, ghost towns, and other sufferings and hurts brought upon communities due to disruption. These social costs and pains have created scepticism and doubt on whether the current technological revolution has anything good for the excluded, the marginalised and the unconnected. Leaders are motivated to innovate by fear – "disrupt or die".

Historically, disruptive innovation has driven significant industrial transformations. For example, combustion engines replaced steam engines, electric light bulbs supplanted paraffin lamps, and automobiles replaced horse-drawn carriages. In the digital age, compact discs (CDs) revolutionised the music industry by replacing audio cassette tapes, although the CD was quickly replaced by music streaming services.

Genuine entrepreneurs and leaders do not set out to disrupt, but disruption is a side-effect of industry recreation and expansion. Disruptive innovations succeed because they deliver consumer surplus, which is higher than what the existing players currently deliver through current market solutions. It reallocates economic resources to where they are deemed to be better used for social good. There are a lot of disruptive opportunities across all sectors of the economy where society's resources are underutilised.

Most industries and sectors in Africa have become dysfunctional due to the continued use of obsolete equipment, practices, and technologies, which are creating inefficiencies, resulting in high operating costs and poor service delivery. Individuals and organisations have thrived within the confines of the old systems and have resisted any disruptive changes that threaten their interests. It is natural for anyone to safeguard their current sources of income. Additionally, for some, the entrenched practices have been ingrained for so long that envisioning alternative approaches seems inconceivable. Path dependency has trapped companies, industrial clusters, and entire societies, unintentionally hindering the adoption of progressive growth models and perpetuating cycles of underdevelopment and poverty.

We cannot go into the future the same way we have arrived here. Given the on-going industrial revolution, the disruptive path provides a way to industrial renewal and economic transformation. The compelling value disruptive innovation unlocks draws new users or consumers who are not incumbents' customers and also traditional incumbents' customers to use the disruptors' product or service more frequently, thus promoting economic growth and social development. There are more people who use ride-hailing services than those who use traditional taxis globally, just as more people use their smartphones to access the internet than computers or laptops. Targeting the underserved segments can unlock hidden avenues for creating new markets, organisational growth, and improved livelihoods over time compared to previous eras.

The Non-Disruptive Pathway

The second pathway to market-creating innovation is non-disruptive. The seminal work of Kim Chan and Mauborgne (2023), published in the book *Beyond Disruption,* broadened the theory and practice of market-creating innovation by bringing non-disruptive innovation into the spotlight. This section on non-disruptive innovation is based on their research and findings.

For a long time, our ideas of market-creating innovations have been centred on disruptive innovation. Since 1997, conversations about new market-creating innovations focused on disruptive innovation. Disruptive innovation became synonymous with market-creating innovation. Yet both disruptive and non-disruptive innovations have been compelling and complementary approaches to creating new industries and re-creating and expanding existing ones. The non-disruptive pathway to new market creation is not new. It has always existed as a business feature but is just hidden. It can be argued that it has been overshadowed by the disruptive pathway, which had been much hyped for a long time.

Given the effects of smart machines that are replacing human jobs and the rise of stakeholder capitalism that is less tolerant of social disruption, non-disruptive innovation has been touted as a sustainable path to creating new markets. It promotes economic growth and generates new jobs without destroying existing ones. It creates a win-win situation because there are no existing market players, whether companies or employees made worse off, as the case is with the disruptive pathway. Non-disruptive innovation provides ample opportunity for growth that is both profitable and rapid because it creates a new cake rather than dividing up the existing one. It is not driven by the need to out-compete rivals and capture a greater share of existing market space. Non-disruptive innovation is a beacon of hope for the excluded, the marginalised and the unconnected.

What Is Non-Disruptive Innovation

Non-disruptive innovation happens when solving an existing or emerging problem creates a new market outside the existing industry boundaries where there are no existing players to disrupt and displace. As a result, economic growth comes with little or no social cost at all. Unlike the disruptive path that involves competing within the confines of the existing industry and stealing customers from existing companies, non-disruptive creates uncontested markets that make competition irrelevant. It pulls in a whole new group of customers who were traditionally noncustomers of the industry, and the market space and size cannot be known in advance.

The idea that non-disruptive innovation creates totally new markets does not entail that it should be a scientific or technological invention that is new to the world. It occurs with a new combination or application of already existing technology, and it does not have to be new to the world but new to a certain geographical region or area. For instance, in 2011, Econet Zimbabwe introduced the country's first mobile money service, Ecocash, yet three years earlier in 2008, Vodacom's Mpesa, a similar non-disruptive innovation, had more than one million active subscribers in Kenya. Therefore, an offering that already exists in one area can be brand new and create a new market when adopted and offered in another area. Applicability of a non-disruptive innovation must not be limited to any social standing, whether low-end or high-end.

Sources of Opportunities for Non-Disruptive Innovation

As with disruptive innovations, non-disruptive market-creating opportunities come from two primary sources: existing but unexplored problems and newly emerging problems. Addressing these kinds of problems with solutions outside the existing industry boundaries is non-disruptive because no industry is in existence to address them. Let's consider each source in depth.

1. *Existing but Unexplored Problems*

All social and economic problems we are facing today are not new in the sense that they are just popping up now. They have been in existence for a long time but have only been unexplored. Think of those problems around you that no one cares enough to address, and everyone takes them for granted because they are not seen as problems worth solving or an opportunity to create valuable commercial mechanisms. This could be attributed to many reasons, including:

- People have intentionally or unintentionally viewed the problem as simply a fact of life.
- People have come to accept the problem as merely the way things ought to be.

- Some well-respected individuals or organisations, at one point in time, tried to solve the problem and failed. Now everyone regards solving the problem as impossible, dampening further efforts to find a lasting solution to the issue.
- Some individuals or organisations have patched up a non-market solution to the problem, which is not only ineffective but also unsustainable.

All these problems and situations provide opportunities for discerning individuals and organisations to create new businesses beyond or outside existing industry boundaries.

2. *Emerging Issues or Problems*

Changes, whether they have already occurred or are currently underway, always provide opportunities for creating something new and different. The overwhelming majority of successful non-disruptive innovations exploit change that has already happened or is underway. Today, some major shifts have already occurred, and some shifts are currently happening all around socio-economic, demographic, environmental and technological changes. These changes are resulting in emerging issues or problems that are very fertile grounds for non-disruptive opportunities. Offering effective and sustainable solutions to one or more of these challenges or problems is a natural avenue to non-disruptive innovation.

How to Identify New Market Creating Opportunities

Having described the two pathways to market-creating innovation, let's go further into how to spot those opportunities and bring them to the surface, whether they are non-disruptive or disruptive. Knowing *where* to look for opportunities is the first step; it gives you the right direction, but knowing *how* to look for the opportunity provides the much-needed focus and alertness to direct efforts and resources.

1. *Direct Experience*

Everyday problems we directly experience, either newly emerging or existing but unexplored, are opportunities for individuals and organisations to uncover pathways to new markets and business success. Paying close attention to these challenges opens doors to unmet market needs or gaps, offering a clear path to developing products or services that directly address these issues. Rather than writing off the problems we directly experience, it is important to alertly focus on them and imagine how solving them can bring real difference to our organisations and communities. If the potential impact is great and meaningful, such focus stimulates creative thinking and pushes you to intentionally explore unconventional solutions to deliver potential value and improve lives.

2. *Observation*

Observing the existing but unexplored or emerging problems and issues around us is another way to unearth new market-creating opportunities. We can create innovative solutions to the problems or issues that other people or communities are directly experiencing. Observing with empathy makes us indirectly experience other people's problems or issues. Empathy is the ability to put ourselves in those people's shoes, understand their plight, share their pain, and be driven to take action to create a non-disruptive solution to their problem.

3. *Scouting*

Scouting for new market-creating opportunities is a purposeful, strategic and proactive approach. This involves, firstly, adopting a problem-solving mindset that forces you to tap into your contacts and networks and even visit different relevant action sites for exploration. You can start with thorough market research to understand industry trends, challenges, and gaps by studying reports and journals to uncover existing but unexplored or newly emerging problems. Employing the following strategies can increase your chances of identifying brand-new problems and issues that can unearth business opportunities:

- Trend Analysis: Leverage data and analytics to understand technological, cultural, and other trends and anticipate shifts in consumer behaviour, demographics, and market demands. Customer feedback is invaluable for this endeavour; conduct surveys and interviews to identify existing and emerging pain points.
- Networking: Attend industry events, courses, and workshops and engage in forums to connect with peers. Gather insights that keep you informed about new developments.
- Collaborative Brainstorming: Work with diverse teams to generate creative ideas and new perspectives on both existing but unexplored and newly emerging problems. Structured processes, such as innovation labs, can help incubate and refine these ideas.

Evaluating Identified Market Creating Opportunities

After identifying a unique market-creating opportunity, the next crucial step is to thoroughly evaluate it. Traditional methods for assessing technical, financial and operational feasibility are not suitable in this context. Conventional techniques, which are based on the resource-based view (RBV) of the firm, are typically designed to determine if a project or opportunity can be pursued using the organisation's existing resources and capabilities. According to the RBV, an enterprise's ability to pursue new opportunities is largely determined by its current portfolio of resources and capabilities. However, this perspective can stifle innovation and entrepreneurship, limiting what a firm can achieve based on its present circumstances.

Therefore, in assessing market-creating opportunities, the objective is not to ascertain the feasibility of solving identified problems or pursuing opportunities with existing resources. Instead, the primary purpose is to determine the value of the opportunity by assessing its potential market impact and broader social benefits. If solving the identified problem has a significant economic and social impact, then it's worth pursuing. Realising the identified opportunity successfully hinges on whether the opportunity is worthy enough to commit to securing the necessary resources to make it happen rather than being limited by current resource availability. More on this idea will be discussed in later sections.

Evaluating a non-disruptive opportunity is more difficult than a disruptive one. With non-disruptive opportunity, you are venturing into uncharted territory, with an unknown market size and uncertain customer willingness to pay. It is difficult to know whether the identified market meets your overall business goals and objectives. To ensure the identified opportunity has a significant economic and social impact, it must resonate with a broader audience beyond just you and your team. The potential market must be substantial enough for the new value to make a meaningful difference. Therefore, it is crucial to assess the market potential of the opportunity upfront before dedicating time and resources.

Gauging the economic benefits and broader societal impact starts by asking: Who else cares about this problem or opportunity? Answering this question requires exploring the problem from the perspective of potential customers or users. Implement a user-centred approach that prioritises understanding the needs and challenges of the end-users. This method helps frame the problem from the user's context, allowing you to identify and focus on the key issue that matters most to them. By doing so, you ensure that your solution is both relevant and impactful, maximising its potential for success. The user-centred approach involves gaining a thorough understanding of the users' needs, pain points, experiences and challenges through:

1. User Research: Conduct interviews, surveys and observations to gather insights about the target audience or potential market.
2. Empathy Mapping: Creating empathy maps to visualise what users say, think, feel, and do helps uncover underlying needs and pain points. Draw a large cross on a board or a sheet of paper, dividing it into four quadrants labelled: Says, Thinks, Does, and Feels. And then, fill in each quadrant with the data collected, ensuring that you accurately capture user quotes, thoughts, behaviours, and emotions.
3. User Personas: User personas are detailed user profiles that capture the characteristics, needs and behaviours of typical users. They are based on data collected from real users and are used to guide design decisions by providing a clear picture of the target audience. Use storytelling techniques to make the personas relatable and memorable.

Framing the Problem or Opportunity Clearly

Based on the insights gathered during the evaluating phase, the next step is to reframe the problem or opportunity clearly. Framing is the process of clearly defining and presenting an identified opportunity in a compelling manner. It entails accurately and persuasively communicating the problem to be addressed, the target market and the unique value proposition you aim to offer to the rest of the team or organisation. Problem framing ensures alignment among team members, provides clarity in direction and enhances the efficient use of resources. By defining the problem accurately, teams can generate innovative solutions that truly meet user needs and deliver meaningful impact. It sets the stage for effective problem-solving, guiding the development of user-centred solutions that address the real challenges faced by stakeholders. The right framing of the opportunity should be inspiring, allowing the entire team to envision the possibility of realising it with confidence and enthusiasm. When an opportunity appears enormous, it also appears impossible. Therefore, frame the opportunity in a way that prevents the team from feeling overwhelmed before the work begins. From the start, everyone should be motivated and committed to pursuing it.

Chapter 5
Tapping into the Opportunity

Many entrepreneurs fail to realise their vision not because they did not identify the right problem for their target demographic but because they could not find a sustainable way of tapping into the identified opportunity. They often succumb to the temptation of rushing into the development phase, aiming to quickly bring their product or service to market without thoroughly analysing the necessary actions, tactics and decisions to bring their vision to life. Tapping into an entrepreneurial opportunity involves taking proactive steps to transform an idea into a sustainable business. The first of these steps is strategic planning and analysis. The goal of strategic planning is not to predict the future but to improve the odds of success in the face of uncertainty and ambiguity. Strategic planning process gives the management team an opportunity to evaluate available strategic options and select one that presents a better probability of success.

Tapping into a market-creating innovation begins with developing a deep understanding of why the opportunity has been overlooked or unaddressed. The opportunity you identified has been concealed from others, which is why it has not been addressed by the existing industry players, in case of a disruptive opportunity or by the industry to which it seems to naturally belong for a non-disruptive opportunity. Research indicates that new market-creating opportunities often remain unnoticed due to the conventional assumptions that underpin the industry's business model. By uncovering and analysing these assumptions, we can develop a deeper understanding of why such opportunities have been overlooked and create a platform for business model innovation.

Uncovering and challenging an industry's entrenched assumptions is crucial for developing a new business model that unlocks market-creating opportunities. This section lays the groundwork for realising the identified opportunity, whether disruptive or non-disruptive. We begin by discussing the concept of business model as a tool for strategising and its significance in unlocking entrepreneurial opportunities. Then, we will explore how to uncover and analyse an industry's assumptions that have concealed the market-creating opportunities you identified and how to challenge them effectively.

Business Model

The business model serves as a strategic blueprint, detailing how a company will operate and achieve profitability through its organisational structures, processes and systems. It is best explained using nine fundamental building blocks, which illustrate the logic behind the company's operations: Value Proposition, Customer Segments, Revenue Streams, Cost Structure, Channels, Key Activities, Key Resources, Key Partnerships and Customer Relationship.

These nine components address the four strategic areas of any organisation, whether for-profit or non-profit: customers, offerings, infrastructure and financial viability. A business model serves as the roadmap for how a company operates and sustains itself in the market, helping it align its strategic goals with operational processes. It does so by spelling out how an insurer processes a claim, a bank determines a business loan, or a retailer manages its supply chain and makes money. In essence, a business model represents a comprehensive framework that outlines how an enterprise intends to generate and deliver value to its target customers. As a result, designing a business model goes a long way in unlocking an entrepreneurial opportunity by providing a strategic roadmap that guides the enterprise from inception to execution. The design process assists in tapping into the entrepreneurial potential in the following ways:

- *Provides Clarity:* The process of mapping and defining the value proposition, revenue streams, target market, and operational plans facilitates more focused decision-making, enabling you to prioritise actions that support growth and competitive advantage. This process brings coherence, focus and direction in terms of what the business stands for, how it will operate and how it will achieve its goals, thus providing a strong foundation for future growth and success. This clarity and foresight can instil confidence in the team and other stakeholders, making them more likely to support and commit to the realisation of the identified opportunity.
- *Facilitates How the Business Integrates into Its Ecosystem:* A well-articulated business model outlines the key resources, activities, and partnerships needed for success. Articulating and outlining these elements assist in defining and refining the business value network. It offers a structured approach to understanding and mapping how the entity interacts with its stakeholders, including key partners and external stakeholders. By systematically addressing these elements earlier, businesses can effectively integrate into their wider ecosystem, facilitating the creation of meaningful synergies that unlock more value and ensure long-term success.
- *Provides a Platform for Additional Analysis:* A business model acts as a powerful tool for testing the feasibility of a venture before fully committing resources. By simulating various scenarios, entrepreneurs can gain valuable insights into critical aspects like the customer value proposition, profit model, key resources, and operational structure. This thorough analysis helps anticipate potential challenges and identify

opportunities and risks, supporting strategic planning and informed decision-making. Such a proactive approach minimises the risk of failure and ensures the business is grounded on a strong strategic foundation.

Overall, a business model is more than just a plan—it is a strategic asset that shapes how a company competes, delivers value, and grows. By designing and fine-tuning business models, a business can differentiate itself, optimise operations, create lasting relationships, and maintain a flexible approach to changing market conditions. These elements collectively drive competitive advantage and help secure a dominant position in the industry.

The importance of the business model design process in unlocking market-creating opportunities and achieving overall business goals cannot be overstated. It provides a structured framework for understanding the current business landscape and anticipating its potential evolution. This process is key to aligning all the core components and systems that will shape the future organisation. While the future is always uncertain and filled with complexities and potential disruptions, developing hypotheses about future trends allows for the creation of adaptive business models. The design and development process is driven by the assumptions made by entrepreneurs or the management team, which play a significant role in assessing risk and return, defining target customers, and determining the scope of the business in terms of both value delivery and capture. These assumptions play a central role in addressing key questions that steer the business model design process, such as:

1. Who comprises our potential customer base?
2. What products or services can we offer, and what drives customer interest?
3. How will we generate and deliver value to our target customers, and how will we capture that value?

4. What strategies will drive profitability for the business?

Addressing these questions encourages the management team to consider how the new venture will deliver compelling value that customers are willing to pay for while also ensuring adequate profitability for the business. By making assumptions about market forces, industry dynamics, key trends and macroeconomic conditions, the team defines the "design space" for developing potential business model options. These assumptions help envision various future scenarios, thereby facilitating the generation of viable business models. Based on pre-defined criteria such as acceptable risk levels or desired growth potential, the team can then select the most suitable option.

To illustrate this point, let's assume a start-up company, XAV, which intends to commercialise its revolutionary vehicle safety system. The company generates three scenarios, each resulting in a different business model:

1. Operating as a manufacturer, embedding its system into vehicles, therefore the model will involve selling the system to original equipment manufacturers (OEMs) such as BMW, Toyota, etc.
2. Functioning as a research and development company, licensing its safety system to vehicle manufacturers.
3. Providing an outsourced service to OEMs and suppliers.

Each option represents a distinct set of challenges and opportunities based on the assumptions made by the management team or owners. Depending on the assumptions the management team of XAV makes, the option they choose influences how the company assess its risk-return and defines its target customers and the scope of its business.

Assumptions form the foundation upon which the entire business strategy is built. These assumptions help the management team navigate uncertainty, shape their decision-making process, and define the direction of the business.

Importance of Assumptions in Business Model Design

Assumptions are beliefs and ideas about various business aspects, including customer behaviour, market trends, costs and revenue streams. They play a critical role in business strategy formulation and are essential because of the following reasons:

- Assumptions serve as the foundation for identifying and defining key elements of a business model, such as the value proposition, target customer segments, revenue streams, and cost structure. Ultimately, these assumptions determine how the business assesses risk and return, defines target customers, and determines the scope of the business.
- Explicit assumptions assist in anticipating potential risks and uncertainties, thus guiding decisions related to investments, engagement strategies and resource allocation. This proactive approach not only mitigates risks but also enhances flexibility, enabling more informed and adaptive decision-making.
- Financial forecasts are built on assumptions about sales volumes, pricing, costs and other financial metrics. These projections are important for securing funding from investors and demonstrating a clear path to profitability.
- Assumptions are hypotheses that can be tested through market research or pilot programs. Validating or revising assumptions based on real-world data refines the business models and enhances reliability.

Clearly, assumptions are indispensable in defining the path forward. They provide a basis for testing ideas, managing risks, and aligning the business strategy with market expectations. However, since assumptions are often speculative, they must be regularly tested and refined to ensure that the business model remains relevant and resilient to changes in the market environment.

Uncovering and Challenging Established Industry Assumptions

Having established an understanding of the role and importance of assumptions in unlocking an entrepreneurial opportunity through the business model design, let's now turn our focus on uncovering and creating an understanding of the existing industry assumptions that concealed the identified opportunity.

The purpose here is not only to discover the assumptions that concealed the opportunity but also to challenge them by unlocking the opportunity for exploitation. Remember, uncovering long-held industry assumptions and challenging them opens the doors to innovative thinking that unlocks the identified opportunity and realising it fully.

Challenging long-cherished industry assumptions is not an easy task because there is a natural human attachment to assumptions born from experience, especially the experience of the challenges encountered and overcome in the past. Yet, recognising these assumptions is crucial to developing effective strategies that unlock entrepreneurial opportunities. The more successful an industry has been, the more tightly people cling to old assumptions. An industry's strongly held assumptions regarding its business model are the product of experience, which is the interpretation of past events. Lessons learned from past achievements and failures guide how risk-return of the industry is currently assessed, its target customers are defined and the scope of its business. These beliefs and ideas cannot be lightly discarded regardless of the fact that experience, even experience gained over a number of years, is not always a reliable guide to future action. Over time, any given assumption usually turns out to be unsound because of constant changes in market conditions, customer expectations and technology. The operating environment is constantly changing, and the lessons learned under one set of circumstances may be completely invalid under another.

Today's challenges may be similar to those of the past, but they are not identical. Blindly adhering to long-held assumptions in a constantly changing world leads to path dependency, which breeds complacency, mediocrity and stunted organisational growth. Economic history has shown that successful companies thrive by embracing change, exploring new pathways and evolving. The sense of security provided by old ways is false and misleading given the increased competition in our globalised markets. Businesses must explore novel ways to connect the dots and unlock new markets. Strong beliefs in conventional industry assumptions blind us from seeing new avenues of growth and prosperity. Innovation and entrepreneurship are all about seeking new ways to connect the dots that lead to the desired future. Old ways are not always the best. Unlocking market-creating opportunities requires boldly challenging an industry's current assumptions.

Challenging our long-cherished industry assumptions does not come easy to all of us. Studies have revealed that most people, especially experts, are reluctant to consider evidence that contradicts their deeply held beliefs and ideas. That is why great innovations came from unlikely sources. The most challenging part is often recognising and articulating those assumptions because they are usually so ingrained in our minds that they seem like objective truths. Without the courage to think openly and develop an independent point of view, it is easy to fall into the trap of taking other people's opinions and assumptions as our own. Asking the following four key questions assists in forming the necessary independent point of view when challenging current industry assumptions:

1. Which assumptions does the industry take for granted but should be eliminated?
2. Which elements should be reduced well below the industry standard?
3. Which elements should be raised well above the industry standard?
4. Which elements should be created that the industry has never offered?

Assumption-Implication Analysis

The Assumption-Implication Analysis is a strategic tool used in decision-making, problem-solving, and critical thinking. Developed as part of the broader field of systems thinking and critical thinking, it has emerged from the recognition that many decisions, particularly in complex environments, are based on assumptions that may not be explicitly acknowledged or examined. It helps individuals and organisations explore the assumptions underlying decisions, actions, or beliefs and understand the potential implications of those assumptions.

The assumption-implication analysis to map the currently held industry assumptions and the business implications of those assumptions provides a more systematic and structured way to challenge them. The tool assists in identifying and deconstructing the existing assumptions of the industry that should have been identified and capitalised on the opportunity you have now identified but could not. By highlighting the key assumptions that relate to the central elements of an industry's business model, the analysis helps reveal why the opportunity was overlooked and reframing those assumptions unlocks how you can now exploit the identified opportunity.

Benefits of Assumption-Implication Analysis

1. *Enhanced Strategic Insight*: By understanding the assumptions behind the current industry business model, leaders can make more informed decisions and develop strategies that are adaptable to change.
2. *Risk Mitigation:* Identifying potential flaws or limitations in current assumptions. Addressing or challenging limiting assumptions allows for the development of alternative plans.
3. *Opportunity Discovery:* Challenging traditional assumptions can lead to the identification of overlooked opportunities, enabling more innovative and forward-thinking strategies.
4. *Improved Communication:* Documenting and discussing assumptions improve transparency and alignment among teams, ensuring that everyone operates from the same understanding.

Assumption-implication analysis is an invaluable tool for enhancing business strategies and models by examining the underlying beliefs that drive decision-making. It empowers business leaders to better anticipate future developments, adapt to market changes, and confidently capitalise on new opportunities.

How the Framework Works

1. *Identify Assumptions*

The first step in using the assumption-implication analysis framework is to identify and articulate the key assumptions underlying the current industry business model. You can create a table with three columns, and in the first column, lay out the three key elements of a business model: risk-return assessment, target customers and business scope. In the second column, articulate the identified assumptions against the corresponding business model element.

2. *Draw out Business Implications*

For each of the assumptions identified and articulated, the next step is to explore the potential business implications of those assumptions. This can be done in the third column of the table you already created. Draw out the corresponding business implication of those assumptions for each of the three elements in the first column. This involves asking "what if" questions to evaluate their impact in concealing the entrepreneurial opportunity you have identified. This helps in understanding the risks, opportunities, and possible unintended consequences.

3. *Challenge and Reframe Assumptions*

Armed with a clear understanding of the identified assumptions and their corresponding well-drawn-out business implications, challenge and reframe these assumptions to develop an alternative business model that exploits the identified opportunity.

The Thesis-Antithesis-Synthesis (TAS) Method

The TAS method is a structured method for understanding and reconciling opposing ideas. It originates from the fields of logic and philosophy and is particularly associated with the dialectical method of German philosopher Georg Wilhelm Friedrich Hegel. It is a framework for critical analysis and problem-solving used in philosophy, debate, and strategic thinking. This method encourages a comprehensive examination of ideas or assumptions by exploring opposing viewpoints and integrating them to create a more refined and balanced conclusion and can be used together with the assumption-implication framework.

The Thesis-Antithesis-Synthesis (TAS) method is useful in conducting the industry assumption-implication analysis by critically evaluating and challenging the core assumptions underpinning an industry's current business model. This approach helps reveal potential flaws in existing assumptions and uncovers how conventional industry assumptions resulted in overlooked opportunities. The TAS method encourages critical thinking, enhances risk management and promotes the development of adaptable and comprehensive multi-faceted strategies.

By rigorously challenging existing assumptions, TAS helps tap into identified opportunities, ensuring that strategies are robust and well-rounded. The TAS process involves three key steps:

1. Thesis: State an existing core assumption relating to the essential elements of the industry's business model.
2. Antithesis: Challenge the stated assumptions with counter-assumptions, which may be the exact opposite of the thesis.
3. Synthesis: Evaluate the implications of both the thesis and antithesis and develop a new approach that integrates insights from both the thesis and antithesis to form a new versatile strategy for unlocking the opportunity.

Practical Steps in the TAS method for assumption analysis include:

1. Brainstorming Sessions: Conduct workshops with key stakeholders to identify entrenched assumptions and potential counterpoints.
2. Research and Analysis: Gather data to support or refute both the thesis and antithesis. This might include customer surveys, market research, and competitive intelligence.
3. Pilot Testing: Implement pilot programs or test initiatives based on the synthesis to evaluate their effectiveness in real-world scenarios.

4. Iterative Refinement: Continuously refine the synthesis through feedback and further analysis to ensure it remains relevant and effective.

Combining the TAS method with Assumption-Implication Analysis offers a powerful way to challenge and redefine existing industry business models, facilitating business model innovation.

Business Model Innovation

Market-creating innovation involves increasing customer value while simultaneously reducing costs. This is achieved by identifying which elements of the existing business model can be eliminated, reduced, raised or newly created. The primary goal is to lower costs by reducing or eliminating certain features or services and enhance or create high-value features or services that do not significantly increase the cost base. This process is facilitated by rigorously challenging current industry assumptions and reframing perspectives, which supports and promotes reimagining key elements.

Business model innovation is key to tapping into the identified opportunity because it transforms an industry's business model by rethinking and redesigning its key elements to drive new value creation, growth, competitiveness, and sustainability. It is at the heart of market-creating innovation, as it goes beyond mere product or service improvements. Business model innovation fundamentally changes how value is created, delivered and captured by reassessing risk-return dynamics, redefining target customers, and expanding or narrowing the scope of business operations through:

1. Connecting previously unconnected parties,
2. Linking partners/ actors in new ways,
3. Introducing new transaction mechanisms.

Business model innovation is transformative for an industry or market. Without a game-changing business model—one that redefines the rules of engagement for incumbents or competitors—an entrepreneurial opportunity can easily go to waste. A notable example is Kodak's acquisition of the photo-sharing platform Ofoto way back in 2001, which gave Kodak the potential to lead the digital photo revolution. Unfortunately, Kodak failed to develop a transformative business model and the chance to create a new market innovation in digital photo sharing ahead of platforms like Flickr and Instagram was missed. Consequently, this opportunity was lost, and Kodak's prominence in the photo industry faded into history.

The success of companies such as Apple, Alibaba, and Amazon is largely attributed to business model innovation rather than product/service innovation. These tech giants have created platform-based business models that generate immense value for all stakeholders, including users. Beyond competing with superior products, these companies have strategically opted to differentiate themselves through distinctive business models.

Having found a way to tap into the identified market-creating opportunity, the next chapter delves into the realisation of the opportunity.

Chapter 6

Making It Happen: How to Realise the Opportunity

Now comes the challenging part. Realising an entrepreneurial opportunity in a cost-effective yet high-value way involves two key components: developing the strategy to unlock the opportunity, as discussed earlier, and executing that strategy. Strategy development is relatively straightforward, as it takes place in a controlled environment with fewer immediate pressures and less internal resistance. In contrast, execution presents unforeseen challenges, such as market shifts and resource constraints.

Making it happen demands more than just a solid plan—it requires exceptional operational and leadership skills. Effective execution involves real-time problem-solving, handling unexpected issues, managing multiple facets simultaneously, and ensuring that all efforts align with the overarching strategic vision. Executing them requires meticulous coordination of people, efficient resource allocation, and overcoming operational inefficiencies.

Strategy execution often means altering entrenched habits, which can provoke resistance and make alignment difficult. Human factors play a significant role; getting people to work together and change their established routines is both challenging and messy. Although clear and effective communication is essential, cross-functional collaboration adds more complexity.

Business school education emphasises that successful strategy execution requires clear alignment with the strategic vision, effective leadership, and strong ownership at all levels. This entails being agile and adaptable in addressing unforeseen challenges. Streamlining communication, efficient resource allocation, and prioritisation of high-impact initiatives are also vital, including continuous performance monitoring and regular feedback to help keep the strategy on track. Building a culture of accountability, investing in team skills, and fostering continuous learning are essential to keep the team motivated and engaged.

However, without a deeper understanding of the three key enablers of strategy execution, focusing on these areas alone may not effectively translate plans into business success. This section discusses the three key enablers that can be used to realise the identified new market-creating opportunity: internal resources, resourcefulness and capabilities, and the right mindset. These three key enablers provide a solid foundation for turning the strategies and tactics into action that unlock the opportunity and bring the product or service to the market.

The Right Mindset

The most important enabler in realising the identified new market-creating opportunity is to operate and lead with the right mindset. Entrepreneurship involves trial and error. The right mindset wins half the battle. Those who lead with the right mindset are more likely to persist in the face of obstacles, refine their strategies and keep pursuing going. There are mainly two types of mindsets that determine how our lives work out: a fixed mindset and a growth mindset.

A fixed mindset manifests as the belief that abilities, intelligence, and talents are static and cannot be changed or developed over time. Leaders and entrepreneurs with this mindset tend to view their qualities as inherent and unchangeable, leading them to avoid challenges, give up easily, and feel threatened by the success of others. It leads them to believe that there is a singular path to success and revolves around the notion of "should" — asking what strategies and technologies "should" be used to make things happen. The focus on "should be" creates a narrow tunnel vision that relies on established industry norms and familiar best practices and processes. It seeks comfort in proven methods but overlooks innovative possibilities that could lead to breakthrough success.

This mindset is limiting when pursuing entrepreneurial opportunities, as it prioritises certainty over what is possible. It stifles creativity and hinders the team's ability to dream, making it difficult to explore and exploit market-creating opportunities. In today's fast-evolving world, where exploration and experimentation are essential, a fixed mindset restricts growth and innovation. Restricting exploration and experimentation creates a culture of compliance and optimisation, which can be effective for executing established strategies within predefined parameters.

However, entrepreneurship and innovation thrive in a culture of experimentation and creativity. Adhering strictly to what has worked in the past or what is already considered "best practice" may lead to the effective implementation of known strategies but falls way short in driving market-creating innovations. In pursuing entrepreneurial opportunities, there are no definite, prescriptive, plug-and-play solutions that guarantee success. Relying on the notion of a clear, singular path to success inhibits creativity and innovation. Emphasising specific criteria or components necessary for achieving identified opportunities limits the flexibility and adaptability needed to explore diverse options and ideas, which are pivotal in dynamic markets.

The important aspect of an entrepreneurial mindset is the growth mindset. Essential for promoting exploration and experimentation, the growth mindset encourages asking, "What strategies and technology could be used to make things happen?" Focusing on "could be" reflects an open, flexible and innovative mindset that acknowledges multiple potential pathways to success. Rather than seeking established answers, a growth mindset inspires thinking outside the proverbial "box", encouraging the curious pursuit of unconventional approaches that may deviate from established and known models. This flexibility empowers teams to imagine and explore possibilities from unexpected sources.

By treating our understanding as dynamic rather than fixed, a growth mindset allows us to embrace new ideas and remain open to change. This approach not only enhances creativity and adaptability but also positions us to be resourceful in realising market-creating opportunities.

While embracing a growth mindset involves greater risk due to the uncertainty and experimentation required, it also presents the potential for higher rewards by uncovering unique value propositions and channels. A "could be" mindset is foundational to a culture of continuous learning and growth because it encourages businesses to experiment with different models and learn from both successes and failures. It emphasises the importance of being able to pivot and adjust strategies as new opportunities or challenges arise, driving long-term success through breakthrough innovations and adaptability.

While a fixed mindset offers stability and predictability, it is only suitable in environments where minimising risk and maintaining the status quo are paramount. It is not conducive to market-creating innovations that require the flexibility, creativity, and adaptability that a growth mindset promotes.

To understand a growth mindset, it is important to recognise its characteristics. A growth mindset embodies the belief that effort and perseverance, both personal and from others, will lead to success. Entrepreneurs and leaders with a growth mindset believe that abilities and intelligence can be developed through dedication, learning, and effort. This belief enables them to embrace challenges and march into the unknown. They are more likely to take calculated risks, explore new opportunities, and tackle challenges head-on rather than stick to safe, familiar paths.

This openness to experimentation helps uncover innovative solutions and strategies for growth. It embraces the journey, whether it is an uphill battle or a downhill sprint. With this mindset, obstacles are opportunities to make things happen. If you can't go through the obstacle, try to go around it; otherwise, go over it. This mindset exudes self-confidence in one's ability to accomplish what others deem impossible.

Entrepreneurship is a leap of faith—faith in your abilities to create new markets and drive growth, even in the face of resource constraints and other obstacles. Entrepreneurs believe that obstacles illuminate new possibilities.

Internal Resources and Capabilities

To make anything happen in life, you need resources and capabilities, whether you want a cup of coffee or build a house for your family. In business, resources are the strategic tangible and intangible productive assets owned or controlled by an organisation. Tangible resources can be financial, organisational or technological and include equipment and production facilities. Intangible assets include the team's expertise, skills and experience, patents, and other intellectual property. Intangible resources primarily derive from human ingenuity and innovation. They are generally more valuable than tangible ones and must be recognised.

Resources alone are not inherently productive and require capabilities to become valuable. Capabilities encompass an organisation's ability to effectively leverage its assets to pursue entrepreneurial opportunities and achieve business objectives. Capabilities are embedded within the organisational structures and managerial processes that facilitate productive activity. Organisational structures and managerial processes define the routines, practices, processes and learning systems within a business. These systems enable the organisation to coordinate, integrate and deploy its assets in a manner that drives the creation and delivery of customer value.

It Is All About the Choices We Make

Research indicates that the relationship between internal resources and capabilities is complex and dynamic. The breadth and depth of an organisation's capabilities, along with the opportunities it unlocks for market-creating innovations, are heavily influenced by its existing resources and strategic choices. These factors shape the organisational structure and managerial processes, which are further refined as the company evolves. To capitalise on new market-creating opportunities, it is essential for internal capabilities and resources to be flexible and continuously change as the business develops and grows. This adaptability ensures that the business must remain well-positioned to innovate and respond to changing market demands. Jeff Bezos and Amazon embody this concept through the "Day 1" mantra, which represents a mindset of continuous adaptation and evolution. He emphasises that for a company to remain innovative and competitive, it must adopt the mentality of being on its "first day" – always focused on learning, staying agile, and embracing new opportunities. This approach ensures that the organisation maintains a sense of urgency and openness to change, avoiding the complacency that can come with success and growth. The idea is that a company must stay resourceful, maintain a start-up-like culture, and avoid the complacency and inertia that can set in as organisations grow.

This notion opposes the dominant paradigm, grounded in Porter's competitive forces model, which perceives strategy as the process of matching internal resources and capabilities with identified opportunities. In this view, commonly known as strategic fit, industry structure plays a central role in determining and limiting the entrepreneurial opportunities a business can pursue.

When confronted with new market-creating opportunities, the idea of matching discourages creativity and entrepreneurship. It limits innovation and creativity. Of course, it is true that the uniqueness of an organisation's existing portfolio of resources and capabilities positions it to pursue and realise the opportunity in a cost-effective yet high-impact manner. However, what a firm can do is not just a function of its existing resources and capabilities; it also depends on what resources and capabilities the organisation chooses to develop and bring together—the strategic choice to develop and acquire new resources and capabilities. For example, Amazon's success is largely attributed to its constant willingness to develop and evolve its internal resources and capabilities. From its early days as an online bookseller, Amazon strategically expanded its technology, logistics, and data analytics capabilities to diversify into areas like cloud computing (AWS), video streaming, AI, and physical retail. This adaptability, driven by the "Day 1" mindset, allowed Amazon to continually innovate and capitalise on new opportunities, fostering a culture of constant learning and agility. Amazon's commitment to evolving its internal resources enabled it to disrupt multiple industries and remain at the forefront of innovation.

The point here is that the successful realisation of market-creating opportunities hinges significantly on an organisation's existing resources and capabilities and its commitment to developing or acquiring new ones. Over time, skills and talent can be cultivated by adopting new organisational and managerial processes, while intangible assets can be built and strengthened through continuous learning and strategic growth initiatives.

New market-creating opportunities can only be turned into reality by building new internal resources and capabilities and integrating them with those that already exist. Over time, the development and integration of new internal resources and capabilities with the existing ones create core competencies, which are the unique strengths and abilities which set the business apart from competitors. They include a combination of skills, knowledge, processes, and technologies that enable a company to deliver distinctive value to customers and sustain competitive advantages. The strategic value of internal resources and capabilities is measured by their contribution to the development of core competencies. How you creatively integrate the available resources plays a pivotal role in making things happen.

Size Doesn't Really Matter

Internal resources and capabilities are foundational for the effective performance of strategic business activities and long-term success. However, the primary determinant of success is not the size of a firm's current resource base but the ability to effectively leverage the available resources to seize entrepreneurial opportunities. This ability involves:

1. Concentrating Resources: Focus available resources on a few clearly defined and consistent goals.
2. Prioritising Efforts: Direct effort and time high priority operational tasks and activities.
3. Maximising Impact: Target activities that have the greatest impact on customers' perceived value. The ability to scale heavily relies on understanding and adapting to customer needs.

By strategically managing resources in this manner, you demonstrate a commitment to taking the small incremental steps necessary to realise the identified opportunity. Doing so allows you to gain momentum, transcend current resource limitations, and leverage human ingenuity and the impact of the available internal resources and capabilities to inspire new possibilities.

The responsibility of leaders and entrepreneurs is not to conduct an internal analysis to match internal resources and capabilities with identified opportunities but to recognise new market-creating opportunities and creatively mobilise the necessary resources to capitalise on them. This entrepreneurial role differs significantly from the managerial duty of sustaining the profitability of existing operations.

This brings us to the next enabler: resourcefulness. Resourcefulness involves finding innovative solutions to bridge gaps in resources and capabilities. Instead of conforming to popular strategic fit, dedicate yourself to achieving market-creating innovation.

Resourcefulness

Resourcefulness in entrepreneurship refers to the ability to creatively and efficiently utilise available resources to solve problems, overcome challenges and seize opportunities. In essence, it is about making the best use of what you have, thinking creatively and being adaptable to achieve set business goals, especially when resources are scarce.

Resourcefulness is the ability to maximise the use of available resources, especially in situations where they are limited or constrained. It goes beyond simply working with what you have—it's about reimagining existing rules, structures, and combinations to find innovative solutions without sacrificing quality. While resourcefulness is often driven by scarcity, its value extends equally to resource-rich environments. In both cases, it enables individuals and businesses to enhance productivity and generate unexpected value, turning perceived limitations into opportunities for growth and innovation.

At its heart, resourcefulness is a boundary-breaking behaviour that transforms constraints into catalysts for creativity. It is the driving force behind many entrepreneurial success stories, where leaders face challenges head-on and leverage them to drive innovation. Resourcefulness means creatively utilising knowledge, expertise, and financial resources, even without direct ownership. It is about recognising untapped potential in what might seem like underutilised assets and deploying them strategically to create new market opportunities and unexpected value.

Whether in situations of scarcity or abundance, resourcefulness helps organisations realise the full potential of their resources, pushing the boundaries of what's possible and creating pathways for new opportunities and growth. Resourcefulness functions as a creative, transformative mechanism that enables individuals and organisations to redefine their resource endowments and reshape their environment to surpass existing boundaries. It allows you to exceed expected outputs from available resources in a manner distinct from concepts like lean manufacturing, which focuses on maximising efficiency within existing operational systems. It operates on the premise that necessity is the mother of invention. When faced with limited resources or other obstacles, people often become innovative, challenging established norms and unleashing the creativity within.

Resourcefulness is closely linked to resilience and persistence. It is not just about surviving with limited resources; it's about finding creative, unconventional ways to make those resources work in favour of the business. It involves not giving up but instead leading with the agency, tapping into human ingenuity.

Kim and Mauborgne identified four key dimensions of resourcefulness that are pivotal to the realisation of new market-creating innovations.

Dimensions of Resourcefulness

The first dimension of resourcefulness in entrepreneurship is the search for knowledge, information or expertise needed to pursue an opportunity. Never underestimate the vast wealth of information available through podcasts, videos, blogs, articles and webinars, all freely accessible online. Conducting research and finding innovative ways to connect the dots has never been easier.

The internet provides unparalleled access to an immense wealth of knowledge, education, and expertise on virtually any topic—from scientific research and technical innovations to thought leadership and industry insights. Resourcefulness means tapping into this vast pool of information and strategically applying it to achieve your goals. By harnessing this readily available resource, you can build and deepen your expertise, allowing you to identify and seize market-creating opportunities. Beyond mere consumption, true resourcefulness involves synthesising knowledge, adapting it to your context, and developing unique solutions. This proactive approach positions you not just as an informed individual but as an expert change-maker capable of driving innovation and creating lasting impact.

The second dimension of resourcefulness entails proactively exploring industries, fields and domains, and current or historical contexts that share structural or functional similarities, though they may differ in specific details. This exploration is aimed at acquiring knowledge, insights and practices that can be adapted to capitalise on your identified market-creating opportunity. This cross-disciplinary approach allows entrepreneurs to draw from a diverse range of perspectives, experiences and expertise enhancing their ability to creatively solve problems and capitalise on identified opportunities.

By examining how similar challenges have been addressed in different contexts, entrepreneurs can uncover innovative solutions and strategies that might not be immediately apparent. Whether it is adopting best practices from a different sector, learning from historical examples or finding inspiration in analogous situations, this dimension of resourcefulness expands an entrepreneur's toolkit and increases the potential for success.

For example, Amazon applied its expertise in scalable infrastructure (originally developed in-house for its e-commerce business) to the tech industry by creating Amazon Web Services (AWS). Being aware, from experience, of the needs of start-ups and enterprises for reliable, scalable cloud solutions, Amazon adapted its internal resources and systems to provide a new revenue stream through cloud computing services. AWS became a market leader by applying principles learned from e-commerce logistics and customer service to IT infrastructure.

Along a similar vein, techniques from the technology sector can inspire advancements in healthcare, while methods used in the hospitality industry can enhance customer service in retail. This cross-pollination of ideas fosters creativity and broadens the range of possible solutions, enabling entrepreneurs to leverage diverse experiences and best practices to overcome constraints and drive success. Embracing this broader perspective enhances the ability to think outside the box and apply unconventional approaches to achieve strategic goals.

The third dimension of resourcefulness involves leveraging the power of collaboration to access collective intelligence and develop innovative, sustainable solutions. This entails recognising the value of building a robust network, actively seeking partnerships and utilising these relationships to advance the realisation of the identified opportunity.

By acknowledging and tapping into the resources and capabilities available outside your organisation or team, you can enhance your efforts through both formal and informal collaborations. Engaging with strategic partners provides access to a diverse pool of ideas, perspectives, and insights, which can significantly propel you toward realising market-creating innovations.

The active pursuit and nurturing of external relationships enable entrepreneurs to harness the collective expertise, resources and experience of their network. This collaboration not only amplifies the potential for success but also cultivates an environment where innovative ideas can thrive. Forming strategic alliances and partnerships can lead to innovative solutions that accelerate the achievement of market-creating opportunities by opening doors to new markets, reducing costs and bridging gaps.

Apple's strategic partnerships with key suppliers demonstrate the critical role of leveraging external expertise to maintain its technological and competitive edge. Collaborating with companies like TSMC (Taiwan Semiconductor Manufacturing Company), Foxconn (Hon Hai Precision Industry Co., Ltd.), and Samsung Display enables Apple to access specialised capabilities that enhance its product offerings. TSMC manufactures custom-designed chips that allow Apple to improve its performance and control over its in-house processors. Foxconn oversees the large-scale assembly of products like iPhones and Macs, ensuring efficient and cost-effective high-volume production. Samsung Display supplies advanced OLED and LCD panels, contributing to superior display quality, despite the competitive dynamics between the two companies in the smartphone market. These and other strategic alliances allow Apple to tap into cutting-edge technology, scale production efficiently, and maintain premium product quality. By outsourcing specific technical functions, Apple concentrates on design, software, and ecosystem integration, reinforcing its market leadership.

Ultimately, a strong network enhances resourcefulness by extending reach, boosting capabilities and driving success through collaborative effort.

The fourth and final dimension of resourcefulness involves uncovering and leveraging existing but underutilised social capital to realise new market-creating opportunities. Social capital encompasses the shared understandings, trust, mutual commitments, and norms that bind people within a community. It influences the quality and extent of social interactions within that community.

Effectively leveraging social capital involves tapping into the collective value of these underused social networks and the collaborative tendencies they foster. By harnessing these connections and the inherent willingness to support one another, entrepreneurs can enhance coordination and cooperation. This not only accelerates the pursuit of new market opportunities but also contributes to both individual and community well-being.

When Econet Zimbabwe launched its mobile money platform, Ecocash, it strategically leveraged existing yet underutilised social capital. The company enlisted street corner shops, commonly known as tuck shops, as Ecocash agents. These agents, who are already well-known and trusted within their local communities, facilitated a smoother adoption of Ecocash countrywide. By offering services through familiar and trusted individuals, Econet Zimbabwe effectively built confidence and ease of access among potential users.

Confidence and Competence

The three enablers discussed in this section build the entrepreneurial confidence and competence necessary to successfully pursue and realise new market-creating innovations. Many have been deterred from pursuing potential market-creating innovations due to limited internal resources and capabilities. However, as demonstrated, individuals and organisations can find creative ways to secure the needed but lacking resources, skills and capabilities only by being resourceful enough and maintaining the right mindset.

The next and final chapter will discuss developments and reasons for Africa to pursue new market-creating innovations, paving the way for a compelling future.

Chapter 7

The Future Is for Us to Create

The COVID-19 pandemic dramatically accelerated the adoption of Fourth Industrial Revolution (4IR) technologies as businesses and societies adapted to unprecedented disruptions. The shift to remote work drove the rapid deployment of cloud-based platforms, artificial intelligence (AI) and machine learning tools, and virtual communication software, ensuring business continuity and enabling social interaction. Supply chain challenges prompted the widespread use of automation and robotics in warehouses and manufacturing, boosting resilience.

In healthcare, the Internet of Things (IoTs) enabled remote patient monitoring, while AI played a pivotal role in predictive modelling, vaccine research, and health communication via chatbots. The pandemic also fuelled a surge in e-commerce, pushing businesses to integrate AI and machine learning for personalised services and contactless payments. Education saw an expansion in EdTech, with schools and universities transitioning to online learning platforms that used AI and immersive reality to offer personalised education experiences.

Cybersecurity advancements followed suit as companies implemented AI-driven solutions to secure data in remote work environments and mitigate rising cyber threats. Cities also adopted smart technologies for public health monitoring and social distancing enforcement, while investments in 5G and infrastructure supported the rise of remote operations. Originally driven by necessity, these technological advancements have become essential to business and societal frameworks, accelerating digital transformation over the years. Each industrial revolution follows the path of an S-curve, illustrating how technologies evolve from early development to widespread impact. The S-curve below depicts the evolution of 4IR technologies from their inception around 1994 to 2020, when they became more accessible and transformative, driving market growth and new operational models. This model offers valuable insight into the trajectory of the Fourth Industrial Revolution (4IR), helping us to map the current status of key frontier technologies and anticipate future trends.

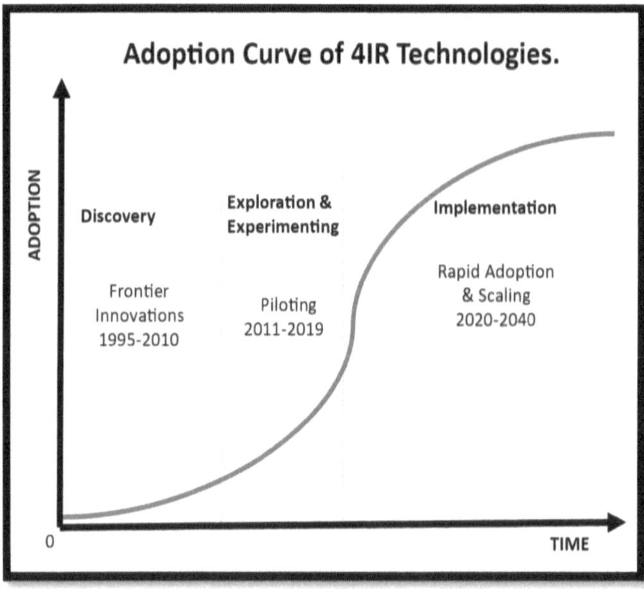

Figure 1: Adoption Curve of 4IR Technologies

Every previous industrial revolution has followed a similar pattern of innovation marked by an initial surge or bubble (discovery), followed by a stall during the exploration and piloting phase and then a period of sustained growth or boom (implementation). The advent of personal computers and the internet led to the first internet companies coming onto the scene in the mid-1990s. Known as the "dot com boom", the internet explosion in this period was a formative period that demonstrated both the immense potential of frontier digital technology. It was a discovery phase in which many dot-com companies operated with unproven or unsustainable business models. Some focused solely on acquiring users without a clear path to profitability, leading to the "dot com crash" in the early 2000s. Despite the crash, the dot-com era left behind valuable infrastructure, technological innovation, and lessons that paved the way for the next wave of internet and digital growth.

The bubble showcased the transformative power of the internet while highlighting the dangers of speculative investment and market hype. This period laid the groundwork for the growth of Web 2.0 in the mid-2000 to 2010, marked by social media, e-commerce and user-generated content.

This growth led to the exploration and piloting phase between 2011 and 2019. During the piloting phase, the broader economy took time to figure out how to best leverage the new machine and business models to catch up with technological innovation. This phase of 4IR technology was marked by significant research and experimentation, laying the foundation for future advancements. This period saw the development of AI and machine learning, focusing on basic algorithms and their applications. IoTs underwent early testing with connected devices through pilot programs, while blockchain emerged in niche projects that expanded its use beyond cryptocurrency. Robotics and automation were introduced in limited industrial settings, marking the beginning of their integration into manufacturing and other processes. These formative years set the stage for more refined and widespread adoption in later phases.

In 2020, the pandemic accelerated the adoption of 4IR technologies, propelling them rapidly through the S-curve. Technologies and ideas previously in exploration and pilot phases were swiftly pushed into full-scale implementation out of necessity, redefining benchmarks for growth and future advancements. We are currently in the implementation stage of the Fourth Industrial Revolution (4IR) technologies—a phase characterised by accelerated adoption, refinement, and widespread integration.

New ideas and technologies that were initially implemented in specific, concentrated areas are eventually spreading and becoming more widely adopted across broader regions and industries. This will continue over the next two decades as industries and institutions that form the pillars of our society—such as banking, insurance, healthcare, education, transportation, law enforcement, and government—will harness the power of advanced technologies and shift their operating models to be rooted in digital solutions. By 2025, the integration of 4IR technologies into businesses is set to advance significantly, fuelled by investments in frontier technologies that are driving substantial enterprise growth. Since 2022, generative AI (Gen AI) has emerged as a dominant force, sparking a remarkable surge in interest and investment. This rapid growth is unlocking new opportunities and fuelling advancements in related fields, such as robotics and immersive reality.

The rapid adoption of frontier technologies such as advanced connectivity, applied AI, cloud computing, and edge computing is driving the scaling of use cases across industries. Natural language interfaces are enabling more humanlike interactions with smart machines, making communication seamless. Businesses now view AI and machine learning not just as tools but as collaborative partners, transforming workplaces into integrated environments where humans and machines work side by side, co-creating in ways never seen before.

For African entrepreneurs and business leaders, the progression of 4IR technology reveals the importance of strategic timing and innovation. By understanding where we stand in the evolution of the 4IR, it empowers us to set the stage for current global trends. All available evidence indicates that we are headed toward the comprehensive build-out of the Fourth Industrial Revolution, and there is a need to make informed decisions about investments and product development. Business leaders and entrepreneurs must carefully choose when to create new markets or adopt new technologies to maximise potential returns. Entering too early, before a technology is mature enough for scalability, can be risky, while entering too late may mean facing saturated markets. Well-timed investments yield significant benefits if aligned with the optimal phase of the S-curve.

The key point is this: when discussing artificial intelligence and other 4IR technologies, the focus is often on their impact on the world we already know. Critics tend to ask, "How many jobs will smart machines destroy?" but the real question should be, "What can this technology improve?" The potential for improvement is vast, and looking beyond 2030, the changes on the horizon are even more transformative. Consider the changes between 2000 and today. The device you rely on at work and at home did not even exist two decades ago, but it is now integral to your daily life. Children born after 2000 look back and ask how we managed without "apps" and social media. This highlights just how rapidly technology is reshaping our world.

The pace of technological adoption presents unique opportunities to drive economic growth, create jobs, and address critical challenges across the continent. As 4IR technologies enter full-scale adoption, the demand for skilled labour and innovative entrepreneurs continues to rise. To meet this need, African governments and business leaders must prioritise talent development and cultivate a workforce proficient in digital technologies, data analysis, AI, and robotics. Collaborating with educational institutions, training programs, and tech hubs is essential to bridge the skills gap and equip the next generation of entrepreneurs with the expertise needed to thrive in entrepreneurship ecosystems.

New Power Dynamics

The idea that the best way to predict the future is to create it is not only cliché but the truth. With advances in technology, shifts in social behaviour and expectations and globalisation, we hold in our hands a powerful tool—a smart device (phone, laptop or tablet) that connects us to vast knowledge sources and expertise, enabling us to solve problems and make things happen at a click. With a smartphone and an internet connection, we can communicate with people anywhere across the globe. The average person now has access to more information than the U.S. government did three decades ago. This widespread accessibility has led to new power dynamics, where anyone with a voice, a smartphone and internet access can influence events and inspire change.

In their book, *New Power: How Power Works in Our Hyperconnected World—and How to Make It Work for You,* Jeremy Heimans and Henry Timms explore the new power dynamics. They explore various real-world examples, such as the election of Barack Obama to the U.S. presidency and the rise of ISIS as a global terrorist organisation, to illustrate how power has evolved with advances in technology and shifts in human behaviour and expectations.

Jeremy Heimans and Henry Timms contrasted the dynamics of new power with those of old power from the industrial era. They noted that old power operated like currency, held by a few individuals who guarded it closely, which means that power was closed, inaccessible and driven by leaders in positions of authority where control was maintained through top-down rules and regulations. In contrast, new power functions more like electricity, generated collectively by many people. Characterised by openness, participation, and peer-driven engagement, new power flows freely and distributes its influence broadly. Like electricity or water, it is most impactful when it surges, spreading widely and empowering those it reaches. The goal with new power is not to hoard it but to channel it effectively.

Events like the Arab Spring and the Black Lives Matter protests highlighted the new power dynamic. African leaders in business, public institutions, and civil society can leverage the significant impact of digital technologies and evolving social norms to harness this power. By facilitating peer-driven participation, they can inspire their teams and organisations to engage with and support the cause for change. I dream of a time when African industries and institutions that serve as the pillars of our society—including banking, insurance, healthcare, education, transportation, law enforcement, and government— leverage the power of digital technology and base their operating models on software and algorithms.

Building a Better Tomorrow, Today

New markets do not emerge by chance; they are created. By harnessing our imagination and digital technologies, the future of our organisations and economies depends on the problems we choose to address and the opportunities we aim to create today. These can be either existing issues that are yet to be fully explored or newly emerging challenges. Africa, in particular, is abundant with market-creating opportunities driven by both longstanding and emerging challenges across various sectors such as education, finance, health, transport and manufacturing.

Dependence on natural resources has historically hindered Africa's economic growth and social development, leading to low incomes, reduced productivity and high levels of poverty across the continent. Transitioning to an innovation-led growth model is essential if we are to build inclusive and resilient economic structures. This shift promotes economic diversification, enhances industry competitiveness, and fosters inclusive growth and sustainable development. Ultimately, it creates new growth opportunities, improves the quality of life, and ensures long-term economic stability and prosperity for people across Africa.

Shifting to an innovation-driven economy unlocks significant opportunities for market-creating innovations. This transition requires the establishment of new industries and institutions that fuel growth and development, reducing reliance on volatile commodity markets and fostering economic resilience. Entrepreneurs play a pivotal role in identifying and pursuing market-creating innovations across diverse sectors, leading to the development of new products, services, and processes that enhance productivity and efficiency. By embracing market-creating innovation, African nations can build a more diversified economy, generate broader employment prospects for their young population, mitigate exposure to external economic shocks and strengthen competitiveness in global markets.

As Africa's population continues to grow, rapid urbanisation is occurring. Young people are flocking to densely populated cities in search of opportunities. This migration is generating significant social and economic opportunities and unprecedented challenges regarding social infrastructure and services for education, housing, mobility, health, finance and resources like food, water and energy. By 2050, it is anticipated that around a billion people will have moved into African cities. These emerging challenges present areas ripe with market-creating opportunities.

Over fifty per cent of the 700 million people worldwide without access to electricity are in Africa. With rapid urbanisation, access to sustainable energy facilitates social development and economic growth. The growing energy demand highlights a significant gap between current capacity and future needs, presenting a vast opportunity for market-creating innovations in the energy sector. These innovations are essential to provide reliable, clean and affordable energy sources, addressing both immediate and long-term energy challenges in the region.

As digital technologies continue to evolve and penetrate every aspect of life, there is a rising demand for individual sovereignty, digital well-being and improved privacy protections. This demand arises from concerns over pervasive digital surveillance, rising cybercrime and the manipulation of personal data to influence elections and politically motivated censorship of news and events. Addressing these challenges presents significant opportunities for market-creating innovations that can create new jobs and promote growth.

Market-creating innovations serve as the conduit for forging a new growth trajectory, as local economies and the continent as a whole are in urgent need to ignite growth and development. We stand on the brink of a transformative era driven by radical new technologies that promise to revolutionise production systems, consumption and economic growth. The key to harnessing these opportunities lies in our collective will to do it. Africa has the potential to achieve economic independence and become a global economic powerhouse through the dedication and effort of its people. The crucial question is not whether Africa's challenges will be addressed or opportunities created, but rather who will lead the transformation and bring to reality the Africa we all want and dreamed of, and do so in an inclusive way that creates sustainable growth and prosperity for all?

Throughout this book, we have explored how market-creating innovations—both disruptive and non-disruptive—are pivotal for promoting growth and prosperity at the organisational level, thus expanding our views on market-creating innovation. The insights shared here go beyond mere intellectual engagement. Moving forward, with clear lenses on market-creating innovations, determination and the application of the frameworks provided here, we can purposefully and systematically identify, pursue and realise opportunities for market-creating innovations. Doing so will drive our businesses, public institutions, and economies towards becoming innovation-driven entities.

www.ingramcontent.com/pod-product-compliance
Lightning Source LLC
Chambersburg PA
CBHW050019170726
48282CB00025B/460
9789348892768